HANDLING AND UNDERSTANDING THE HORSE

HANDLING AND UNDERSTANDING THE HORSE

MARCY AND TONY PAVORD

SWAN·HILL
PRESS

Acknowledgements

The authors would like to thank everyone from whom we have gained knowledge – great or small – along the way on our lifetime's journey with horses; all the trainers and experts mentioned in this book and many others whose knowledge is passed on from one enthusiast to the next. The more you learn about horses the more you learn that there is nothing new, but there is always more to learn. For help in producing this book, we would especially like to thank Becky Telfer, who works with us and patiently posed with the horses while we took photo after photo; also Val and Chloe Jones, Sally Tottle, Alison Bennett, the 1998 British Intermediate Endurance Team, Alex Nix, Eric Mole, and the 1987 British Endurance Team.

Dedication

To the horses of the Tawmarsh Stud, who have provided us with
endless fascination:
Rosy, Tara, Tamarisk, Tory, Ria, Merlin, Elf, Desert Rose, Rojo, Rafiki,
Mimi, Tarina, Kelly and visitors Kashala and Chatelaine.

Copyright © 1999 Marcy Pavord and Tony Pavord

First published in the UK in 1999
by Swan Hill Press, an imprint of Airlife Publishing Ltd

British Library Cataloguing-in-Publication Data
A catalogue record for this book
is available from the British Library

ISBN 1 85310 967 3

Typeset by Servis Filmsetting Ltd, Manchester
Printed in Italy.

Swan Hill Press
an imprint of Airlife Publishing
101 Longden Road, Shrewsbury, SY3 9EB, England
E-mail: airlife@airlifebooks.com
Website: www.airlifebooks.com

Contents

Introduction

Horse riding is increasingly popular as a leisure activity, attracting many people with no prior knowledge of horses. The attraction may begin as a stylised ideal, from watching top equestrian sportsmen and women, or horses on film or television. The reality often proves rather different, when it becomes apparent that the newly acquired horse – large, powerful and very real – has a mind of its own, with an agenda based on its natural instincts and characteristics that has nothing to do with the wishes of its proud new owner. Some horses, such as older 'schoolmasters', or ponies that have seen it all before, may be basically uncomplicated and easy to manage. However, the vast majority of horses and ponies are more complex, with individual personalities and behaviour developed from their experience of life so far. The advantage of this adaptability of nature is that the horse can be trained and a wonderful partnership built up with an understanding owner. The downside is that the owner must know how to persuade the horse to co-operate.

Between the heights of scientific theory, research and study and the basics of traditional, sometimes hidebound and inflexible, methods of horse coping, lie the problems, frustrations and lack of effective, practical knowledge of how to deal with them that face the non-professional horse-owner every day. This book is for the owner/rider for whom the advice 'consult an expert' or 'leave that to the experts' is not good enough. In the horse world it often seems that 'experts' are some mythical race apart, who have achieved their status by some kind of divine intervention. But if no one shows us the way, how can the rest of us hope to achieve any kind of expertise in our own dealings with horses?

There is no reason why a concerned, intelligent person cannot achieve the level of knowledge, competence and understanding necessary to develop a thoroughly rewarding partnership with whatever horse they happen to own. This goes well beyond the basics of stable management and level of riding which equates to little more than not falling off that the novice rider is often encouraged to accept.

This book, therefore, is an attempt to explain why horses behave as they do and to show how scientific theory and psychological understanding can be put to practical effect. It does not follow any one 'school' or 'method' of horse training. For the most part, it is the result of my husband Tony's and my combined experiences of two lifetimes of breeding, training, riding and caring for horses. Along the way, we have taken in many valuable and helpful ideas from various trainers who are genuinely 'experts' in their field and we have acknowledged them as appropriate. Some we know personally, in other cases we have absorbed their teaching from books, demonstrations, etc.

To sum up, we hope this book will tell you all the things you need to know about horses that conventional books and teaching do not tell you. Finally, we wish you a very happy partnership with your horse.

Chapter 1

The Horse, Its Nature and Its Relationship with Other Horses and with Humans

Put yourself in the horse's hooves

The relationship we should all like to have with our horses is one of trust and harmony, so that we can relax in each other's company and achieve mutual satisfaction from our shared activities. The key to success in all your dealings with horses and ponies is to learn the knack of putting yourself in the horse's hooves to such a degree that it becomes habit.

The paralysis of fear

To begin accomplishing this, it is necessary to overcome any fear you may have of the horse. Why? Because fear is the ball and chain, the brick wall, the paralysing drug that overrides our ability to be objective. What it does to us, it also does to the horse, with the additional factor that the horse may not be afraid at all until it senses our fear. Researchers have suggested that because the horse has restricted verbal language, some or all of its other senses may be heightened. Observation shows, so often that it can be taken as fact, that a nervous handler creates nervousness in the horse.

The horse's fear has the same outcome as our fear does for us. It triggers the 'flight or fight' mechanism, the horse's natural response to danger, whether actual or perceived.

Very few horses willingly fight, so if they cannot flee and their perception of danger persists, their most likely reaction is to become increasingly frustrated and agitated, making the risk that they might unintentionally hurt the handler a real one. Very quickly, horse and handler enter a downward spiral where the more frightened the handler, the more agitated the horse and the more agitated the horse, the greater the handler's fear.

Respecting the differences between horse and human

Fear of the horse has no place in successful horse handling. You must respect your horse for what it is and give it the opportunity to learn to respect you. How can we develop this mutual respect without fear? First, let us look at some ways in which horses and humans are different, and some ways in which they are similar.

The horse's list begins with ways in which the

Horses are designed for sudden flight.

The newborn foal has to meet all kinds of new species.

Horse	Human
Large size	Comparatively small size
Heavy	Light
Strong, powerful	Weak
Fast (four legs)	Slow (two legs)
Good hearing	Poor hearing
Good scent recognition	Poor sense of smell
All round vision (prey animal)	Forward vision (predator)
Social animal (hierarchies)	Social animal (hierarchies)
Communication by touch	Communication by touch
Limited digital dexterity	Extensive digital dexterity
Limited verbal language	Extensive verbal language
Limited time awareness	Extensive time awareness
Limited power of reason	Extensive power of reason

horse is superior to the human and ends with those where the human is superior. In the middle are two important areas of similarity and these form the basis upon which our relationship with each other can be developed. Both are social animals, living in family groups and understanding the hierarchies that form in such groups, and both understand touch as a means of communication.

Other attributes come into the equation. For example, researchers have studied the horse's ability to vocalise and we understand the meaning of the various equine sounds. However, horses do not have the wide vocabulary that would enable them to communicate verbally as humans do. Their concerns are limited more closely to the necessities of life. Your horse does not need to know how to discuss the latest interest rates, book a holiday or programme a computer.

However, the ability to see behind you, to hear a threatening sound more quickly than a human, or to sense danger may well be useful if you share your environment with a mountain lion. Two acquaintances of ours were riding quietly when their horses suddenly bolted. The riders had heard nothing, yet no sooner did the horses move than a heavy branch fell into the path behind them. Was it some sixth sense, or did the horses simply hear the threat of cracking wood in time to escape?

The horse's size, weight and strength can be intimidating. We must, of course, respect these things, but we must also realise that the horse does not normally seek to use its physical superiority aggressively. The only time this is likely is when stallions challenge one another for a mare or harem. Even then, noise and threatening attitudes often resolve the situation without a fight.

Only a very seriously traumatised horse will use its superior physical power deliberately against a human being. Humans are far more likely to be injured simply through being in the way of a worried, excited, frightened or distracted horse. They fail to create a situation where the horse respects the human and understands how it is expected to respond, or the horse is simply unaware of the effect of its power, strength and speed of action in comparison to the weakness and slowness of the human.

It is not so much the horse's actual use of its size and strength which frightens human handlers, but

the potential threat to use them. This happens frequently, in many ways, which we will look at in detail later. What we need to understand is that this is normal behaviour in a social hierarchy where members of the group naturally compete with each other in varying situations and with varying results. For example, in human society, businessmen compete for promotion over one another. In poorer societies, mothers may compete for food for their families and, in history, armies fought for power. In the same way, horses compete for the right to the best food, to be first at the water hole and, in the case of males, for the best or most females. Youngsters play competitive games to see who is strongest or fastest. In all these cases threat behaviour is the basis of the competitive challenge. How far that behaviour is allowed to develop depends upon the determination of the challenger in relation to the reaction of the challenged.

Dominance and submission

Observation of any group of horses will show how this system works. We studied an 18-year-old Thoroughbred mare, her 2-year-old castrated son, a 14-year-old Arab mare and her yearling colt, reintroduced to the group after weaning. The Arab mare quickly made her dominance over the others obvious. When the other mare or the young gelding approached her, she snaked her neck, pinned back

As the youngster is led in from the field, her family follows with interest.

The weanling mouths submissively at his older playmate . . .

. . . . but Merlin's bared teeth and ears back gesture shows that he does not want to play.

her ears and chased them away. If they persisted, she lashed out in their general direction. Before retiring, this mare was a fiercely competitive endurance horse. At feeding time, she kept the others, including her own youngster, away from the fence until she was fed. The older broodmare quickly gave in to the younger mare's dominance and kept her distance. When waiting for food she would stale, or roll, a form of 'displacement' activity that pretended indifference to the situation. She was also subservient to her 2-year-old son, but not to the other mare's yearling colt. Interestingly, she adopted a protective role towards this youngster, whose own dam was often indifferent to him, and often kept him company.

It used to be thought that a mare that exhibited such domineering behaviour in the wild would be the decision-maker, the lead mare who decided when to move the herd to new pastures. It has since been observed that this is not necessarily the case and many different factors are involved in the social interaction of horses that form a herd. However, the stallion does not lead, but follows, ensuring that no one gets left behind.

In our relationship with our horses, we must take the roles of both the dominant party and the lead mare. This means we must refuse to be intimidated when our horses challenge our leadership and, further, we must lay down challenges of our own, which we do whenever we ask our horses to go somewhere, do something, or to accept something being done to them.

We hope that from the above, you understand that when your horse challenges your leadership, this is not deviant or 'bad' behaviour, but natural behaviour. Your horse is just telling you 'I do not want to do this'. It is then up to you to demonstrate in a way that it can understand and without undue aggression that you are the leader, it is the follower and therefore it must accept your authority. Otherwise it will challenge you with increasing frequency. Since riding is something that is not natural to the horse, and something that you want to do when it may not, you will end up not riding at all.

Fortunately for us, most horses quickly accept the determined and correctly communicated challenge of human authority and submit to the role that we desire them to play. This is the essence of the young horse's training. Each new step, the introduction of tack, grooming, learning to lead, lunge and be backed, are all small challenges to which the horse must submit. They must be broken down into small, logical steps, so that the horse understands them. Otherwise it will become fearful

Brother and sister indulge in mutual grooming.

Rosy is giving good notice that she intends to drive another horse away from a feed bucket. Her head is lowered and snaking forward, her ears are back and her walk is determined.

However, she shares her own bucket with her foal.

and confused in response to the 'flight or fight' mechanism – a state in which it is incapable of learning anything.

Why do the followers in a herd submit to the authority of a lead mare? Why do they not simply ignore her and do their own thing?

Often, they are younger family members, who may remain with their mothers for up to two years. Larger groups also include unrelated mares and we can deduce that they obtain some benefit from their submission. The most obvious for a grazing herbivore is that there is safety in numbers. As the species evolved, those that did not learn this lesson and pass it on to their descendants, did not survive. We can also surmise that over the millennia they have discovered that the leader knows the best foraging areas, water supplies, shade, shelter and dust wallows. In other words, in return for their submission, they gain rewards of safety, sustenance and other things that keep them healthy and alive.

Challenge and reward

This must become part of our training system. We lay down a challenge and ask the horse to submit, without fear and without fleeing or fighting. When it does, we offer a reward.

Learning by association

'Ask a little and praise a lot' is a familiar tenet of horse training. Effective training also recognises that horses learn by association. As an example, watch a horse that has been put in an electric fence corral for the first time. The fencing does not appear very substantial and the horse wonders if it can get out, but is aware of a strange ticking noise. Cautiously, it reaches out and touches the fence with its nose. Within a couple of seconds, it bites! The horse jumps back in alarm, recollects itself and realises it is not really hurt. It might have another go, just to see if the original bite was a one-off, but soon learns that if it touches the fence, it bites. In time, a clever horse will learn that the fence only bites if it is ticking, and will only respect it if the current is actually turned on.

Learning by association only happens when the effect is immediately linked with the cause. Reprimands must be instantaneous in response to the misdeed, ideally within half a second, or the horse will not relate your action to whatever it did wrong and will just be confused. Quick reactions and determination are attributes of dominant personalities. Hesitation and uncertainty are attributes of submissive personalities.

Communicating with the horse

We have said that when you ask a horse to do something, it must be able to understand what you want. As shown by the table on page 8, the horse's perception of the world, using its senses in different ways and to different degrees from humans, is very different from ours. Therefore, we cannot explain something to a horse in the way we would explain it to a human. Nor can we expect the horse to understand us by analysing our behaviour – it does not have the necessary command of language. The horse can only relate what it sees, hears, smells and feels to its situation right now, and if that is alien or strange, it will not be trusted until it becomes familiar and proven to be safe.

By observing and analysing how the horse perceives the world and how it reacts to varying stimuli, we can discover how to communicate with it in a way it can understand. To do this we must employ the attributes listed, in which humans are superior to horses.

First, we can use language to describe what the horse does, what we would like it to do and ways in which we might encourage this. Second, we can use our hands to make adjustments to the horse's environment in ways which give us a tremendous amount of power over it – putting it in a stable, haltering and leading, tying up, etc. Third, we can appreciate the passing of time and the consequences of action. For example, we know that if the horse will not go past the pig farm, we will not be home in time for tea. The horse does not have this awareness of time passing and this is a major stumbling block encountered by less experienced handlers. Finally, we are able to reason what the result of any activity might be. We might think, if I am late putting the horse away, I will be late for my meeting. If we allow ourselves to be frustrated by this situation and thus mishandle it, we permit an ongoing problem to develop. However, if we use our power of reason in advance, we can avoid or solve the problem. For example, we can avoid it by deciding 'I will not go past the pig farm in case my horse does not like it and I end up being late.' We can solve it by deciding 'I will go past the pig farm on Saturday morning, when I have plenty of time and it will not matter if I am late back.'

The horse, of course, does not have these human powers of language, manual dexterity, and awareness of time and consequences. All it knows is that pigs are a new and terrifying kind of monster. If it could visualise that far ahead, which it cannot, the horse would decide that tea in an hour's time is irrelevant when you are in immediate danger of being eaten by a pig! The solution in fact consists of desensitising the horse to the presence of pigs, so that it no longer fears them.

Understanding horse senses

How do the horse's senses cause it to perceive the external environment? How does it use them to communicate with others, perform its habitual actions and fulfil its daily needs?

Vision

The horse's evolved physiology equipped it to be a wandering grazer and browser, and to survive in an environment where other animals developed as predators. Its eyesight provides a wide range of mainly monocular vision, with an area in front where the range of both eyes overlaps to give binocular vision. Immediately in front of the nose is a blind spot. The horse is also blind directly behind itself, for a rather wider space, and its upward and downward sight is also limited. One morning our three fillies all turned their heads at the same moment towards the far fence. They had spotted something moving in their field and swung their heads in unison so that the intruder came within their binocular range, where they could focus on it more clearly. Once they established that it was a fox, and not dangerous, they took no further notice.

If your horse spots something either high or low as you ride along, you will notice how it tilts its head to bring it into sharper focus.

Rojo has spotted the newly delivered fencing rails and stops to stare. Note the tension through his body.

Becky calmly encourages him to take a closer look.

The power of human hands: Merlin has submitted to Becky's hands fitting him with all this tack, and now he obeys both her verbal and physical instructions.

Head up, ears pricked, Tammy's attention is on something she has spotted in the distance.

Hearing

We have already touched on hearing and know that horses can hear higher noises and distinguish distant sounds better than humans. How often has your horse suddenly become alert on a ride, long before you hear or see another rider on your route? The ears are also highly expressive indicators of mood.

Pricked ears indicate alertness, eagerness and anticipation. Ears that are cocked in varying directions indicate that the horse is listening to something, or trying to hear it better by pointing an ear towards the sound. For example, a horse with its attention on a handler at its side may have the nearest ear cocked back towards the person to keep

In the middle of eating, Tammy has heard something move behind her and although she feels secure in her stable, her ears have turned back to listen and her jaw has momentarily stopped moving.

track of their movements. A dozing horse's ears may be relaxed and droopy, while ears flattened backwards against the skull indicate anger or aggression. However, ears held down and back may also reflect concentration and submission in the working horse.

Smell

Horses, like many animals, use their sense of smell to identify things, such as other horses, strange creatures, or edible or inedible objects. It seems that they can follow other horses and find water by smell. By trapping scent-laden air in their Jacobson's organ, using the expression called Flehmen, which closes the nose, they can analyse smells more precisely. Behaviour may be associated with particular smells. The smell of mints may encourage your horse to nuzzle your pockets, while the scent of an in-season mare's urine will excite a stallion. Unfamiliar scent on a familiar person –

such as perfume – might confuse a horse.

Taste

Taste is linked with smell and is most likely to be of concern to the handler when the horse refuses to eat food laced with medicine. As a generalisation, horses like sweet tastes and dislike bitter ones. However, not all sweet-tasting foods are automatically accepted. Most horses love carrots but we have one which refuses to have anything to do with them and once, when I sliced some spare apples into the fillies' feed, one carefully left all hers in a corner of the manger. It was the first time she had encountered this new taste and she did not have the confidence to trust it. If she had seen and smelt her friends eating theirs, she would probably have risked following suit and discovered a new delicacy. The dislike of bitterness may have safety implications, since many poisons have a bitter taste.

This three-year-old colt is scenting a mare in season. He raises his head and rolls his upper lip in the expression called 'Flehmen' to examine her scent more fully.

Touch

Touch is something we use all the time without conscious thought and so do horses. Certain areas of the body are more responsive to touch (i.e., have more nerve endings) than others. Our fingertips are very sensitive and we use our hands for most of our everyday tasks. The soles of our feet are similarly sensitive and if the modern world and climate allowed us to go barefoot safely, our feet and toes would be more useful and well developed than they are in most people today.

Horses' feet, the equivalent of our toes and fingertips, are not very sensitive externally, being formed of horn. However, the coronary bands and pasterns are sensitive and horses, like all animals that depend on flight to escape danger, are very much aware of anything happening to their lower limbs. This has implications when a horse first learns to have its foot picked up, as the instinct not to do so is very strong. It also explains why a horse with its foot caught in wire or a hole may panic and make the situation worse in the attempt to free itself. Sometimes, however, training and confidence in humans will overcome instinctive reflex. We had one young mare with the habit of pawing the wire fence while waiting for her feed. One morning soon after she was first shod, I saw her from a distance with her forefoot on the fence. Half an hour later, when I returned with her breakfast, she was in exactly the same position. I saw that she had caught a strand of plain wire between her shoe and hoof. If she had panicked and jumped back, or given a good tug, the wire would have snapped and she would have been free, but clearly she had figured out that sooner or later a human would come and sort her out. This mare was an Anglo-Arab and the Arab breed is well known for its intelligence and sense of self-preservation.

Where the horse cannot use its hooves, it often uses its lips and teeth. The muzzle, including the whiskers, is another very sensitive area loaded with nerve endings. A further spot is the intercostal nerve, just behind the shoulder at the girth, conveniently close to the point where we give leg aids.

Touch plays a major part in how we communicate with horses. We use our hands on the reins, our weight on the back, our legs on the sides and do many things when dismounted. The success of our training methods depends greatly on the ways in which we use touch and we shall look at many of these in more detail later.

Conformation

The last aspect of physiology that we shall consider is conformation. Although it is not one of the five senses, it can affect the way a horse reacts to training. All horses are of the species equus caballus. However, there is enormous variety among the hundreds of breeds and types of horse and pony that form its members. It must be said that some are more suitable than others for adaptation to riding. Within breeds and types, there is further disparity of conformation (the shape and size of the various body parts and the way in which they are put together). Many problems which occur with ridden horses can be attributed, at least partly, to them being asked to do things for which their bodies are not suited and we will look at this subject more closely in Chapter 8.

Communication between horses

How do horses communicate with one another?

By sound

When we move a group of horses to a new field, they often spend some time neighing to others in different fields. It is as though they are saying, 'Hey, you lot! We've moved.'

A horse greeting another at a distance will neigh loudly, then stand rigidly at attention, with head raised and ears pricked, while it concentrates on listening for a response. At such a time, it does not want to pay attention to its rider, which is unfortunate in the middle of a show. For this reason, riding horses are often discouraged from

greeting their friends. Most horses learn to accept it and concentrate on their work, but problems arise when two horses have become very attached to each other. We have one that behaves perfectly on a trip alone, but if her companion goes too, she becomes extremely upset if separated from her by more than a few yards. This horse, after weaning, spent many months without other equine company and her behaviour now might just reflect the anxiety and stress she experienced being isolated as a weanling.

Horses that live together or are members of the same family recognise each other's neighs and the sound carries a considerable distance, so the neigh is important in keeping track of the whereabouts of the individual's companions or herd.

The nicker is a more intimate form of communication, used by a mare to her foal, by close friends when they come into immediate contact and as part of the courtship routine. A horse that knows and trusts you may nicker when you approach it, especially at feeding time! It occurs when horses are concentrating on each other at close quarters and may vary in tone from welcome to warning.

When horses that are uncertain of one another meet, an initial nicker may be followed abruptly by a squeal, which is a strong form of warning and may also signal resentment and rejection. The squeal may be accompanied by striking out with a forefoot, especially by mares. Squeals may occur in mock fights, in anger or irritation and during courtship.

The stallion's scream of challenge is probably more prevalent in film and literature than in real life. The scream is the ultimate verbal expression of equine rage, whether emitted by stallion, mare or gelding, and whether in a sexual or other connotation. It should have no place in the normal communication of horse and human, and if it does occur, there is a serious problem in hand.

Horses snort loudly when surprised or astonished by something strange. The sound is accompanied by the horse drawing itself up to be as impressive as possible, evidently to intimidate the subject of the alarm. The situation occurs when the horse is not frightened enough to run, but is thoroughly alerted – and alerts its companions – to the possible threat. When a horse snorts, its whole body vibrates with the tension of readying itself for fast and violent action should the threat develop into real danger. What happens next depends upon the behaviour of the handler, rider or other horses, or of the threat object.

Some horses, particularly highly bred ones, exhibit the sound called 'high blowing', a series of snorting sounds made in rhythm with their breathing, especially when cantering. It is usually a sign that the horse is feeling good.

Other noises include grunting, when the horse is making an effort, especially against its own will; sighing, just as a human might and, again, associated with having made a strong effort; and groaning, which may be associated with pleasure, as when stretching out in the sun, or with pain.

All the sounds made by horses are significant, if the handler understands them. It is well established that the horse will respond to the voice and even learn to obey vocal commands, but the handler must be aware of the effect of different types of sounds, use them appropriately and consistently and be able to differentiate between soft, firm and harsh tones.

By body language
Horses communicate by smell and touch as well as sound. We can communicate in return by touch and sound, and be passive communicators by allowing them to smell us. Another means of communication, which the horse uses continuously, is posture, that is, body language. Appreciating this is probably the most important key to gaining the horse's respect and its attention to the learning process. Many owners have difficulties because they do not realise that this is a two-way process. They may be aware of what the horse's body language means to them – for example, if it lays its ears back and snakes its head towards me, it is going to bite – but they are unaware of what their own body language means to the horse. For example, if you raise your hand sharply in front of the horse's face, intending to stroke it while you are perhaps chatting to someone else, how is it supposed to know that you are not going to hit it? That fast movement of your hand into its blind spot is perceived as a threat.

Motivation
We need to understand what motivates the horse's normal behaviour in order to equip ourselves to handle, ride and train them.

The first priority of all animals, including the human animal, is survival. Requirements for survival are eating, drinking, sleeping, exercising and coping with danger, which in the horse's case means fleeing from it. If you want to gain your horse's attention, you must first take care of its need for these things. It cannot concentrate on what you want when it is hungry, thirsty, tired, too fresh, or frightened.

The second priority is procreation and that means reproducing the individual's own genes. At certain times the need to mate totally preoccupies the mind of a healthy stallion or a mare in season. Handlers overcome the inconvenience of these natural urges in several ways, the most obvious being the gelding of colts. Animals that are castrated before sexual maturity rarely develop stallion-like behaviour. However, animals that are castrated after becoming sexually mature may continue to exhibit a degree of stallion-like behaviour, especially if previously used for breeding, so equine male behaviour does not depend entirely on physical factors.

Training plays a strong part in controlling stallion behaviour, as the horses learn the difference between stud and ridden work and behave accordingly. A ridden mare in season may be less willing, more easily distracted and exhibit changes of mood and temperament towards other horses and humans, but this is not usually a problem unless competition performance is affected, in which case hormone treatment to control the oestrous cycle can be given.

Learning equals play
By the time they reach maturity, horses learn many things – which foods are safe to eat, how to behave in a social group, how to escape from danger, how to cope with various hazards. They learn by exploration, trial and error and, when very young, by copying their mothers. To learn anything there must be motivation, some of which comes from physical need, such as hunger. The rest comes from curiosity, the need to be active and explore the world, to meet challenges and, in fact, to play. The

Play fighting is a regular activity for young colts.

word play has many definitions, but one is 'to perform acts not part of the immediate business of life but in mimicry, or rehearsal, or in display'.

We have noted that horses learn by association and that association with a reward reinforces the correct response to a challenge. Now we can add that repetition of a particular action improves its performance, that is, practice makes perfect.

Young colts indulge in mock battles in practice for their later life as grown stallions. All young horses practise many other things in the form of play. These include facing up to fancied dangers, such as a strange-shaped rock, and then running away, or playing with objects such as twigs or buckets, or teasing their elders, or just bucking, jumping and racing to try out their developing bodies.

Riding a horse and handling it on the ground can also be defined as 'play'. In past centuries, when horses were vital to human society in terms of transport and haulage, the play had a serious purpose. Today, we use horses for pleasure rather than work, so we should be able to spend time enjoying our interaction or 'play' with them. 'Play' in this sense means developing communication through the various means at our disposal, to create a partnership of mental and physical harmony. Thus, when we ask the horse to move, by voice and touch or both, it understands what we want and

willingly complies. Touch can mean the pressure of your fingertips on its skin or the transfer of weight through your seat from one part of its back to another, or the vibration of your hand through the leadrope or rein.

Types and breeds

There are hundreds of horse breeds in the world, each with its own characteristics. For the purposes of handling and riding, we need to know whether the horse is a hot-blood, a cold-blood, or, as most are, somewhere in between.

'Hot blood' refers to two specific breeds, the Arab and the Thoroughbred and their exclusive cross, the Anglo-Arab. These breeds are known for their speed, stamina and courage. They are intelligent and quick to learn – both good lessons and bad ones! They make wonderful riding horses when trained sympathetically and ridden with sensitivity. Mishandled, they can become extremely difficult. The Thoroughbred is bigger, stronger and usually more inclined to panic when confused or frightened than the Arab. The Arab has an incredibly strong sense of self-preservation and will not be pressurised into doing something it does not understand or trust. There is no better horse for a genuine horseman than the Arab, but if you are not prepared to spend time gaining your horse's trust and co-operation, or to

19

A Welsh Mountain pony, ideal for a child.

give and take, it is not for you.

Cold-bloods developed as draught and heavy transport horses. Their value lay in their strength rather than in their mental capacity, while docility was a prime consideration when selecting and breeding such large, heavy animals to work with humans. Shire, Clydesdale and Suffolk Punch are the breeds native to Britain and although they can be ridden, their main use is in harness.

Warmblood, although it generally calls to mind the continental riding breeds such as the Hanoverian, Dutch Warmblood, or Selle Français, is a generic term defining a mixture of hot and cold blood in the breeding of the horse concerned. In Britain, the term half-bred is usually used to denote a horse that is half Thoroughbred and half derived from other breeds, whether draught, native pony, or unregistered stock. When selectively bred, such horses are of good riding quality (derived from the Thoroughbred) with a calmer temperament (derived from the draught stock). They make up the bulk of horses used for showing, competing and leisure riding. However, because they derive from many different breeds of varying characteristics, they also vary enormously in character and temperament and it cannot be assumed that every half-bred, or part-bred horse or pony will react in the same way. In the words of a livery yard owner who also buys and sells horses for clients: 'They want a horse of seven or eight years old, that is calm and quiet to ride, with perfect manners and a snaffle mouth, regardless of their hands. It must do a bit of everything, including jumping, without putting a foot wrong, must be bombproof in traffic, but be forward going and not dull!'

People who specify such requirements, as this horsewoman knew, will never be satisfied. Horses are not machines and do not behave with precision. They do not stop developing and changing once their basic training is complete; everything that happens to them each day has an effect on how they behave and react to people. In addition, the ridden horse is only 50 per cent of the equation; the rider has an equal or, perhaps, greater influence on what happens. This is why a horse that will go perfectly well for one rider may be completely confused by someone less skilled and why new owners sometimes have such apparently insurmountable problems.

The nine British native breeds offer considerable

choice to the first-time owner and, if you want to progress to something more ambitious later on, a good pony will always be saleable, or can be diverted perhaps to driving in harness. There are many books detailing the characteristics of each breed, and studs will be only too delighted to show you their stock to help you make up your mind.

If you are buying your first horse or pony, do not be rushed into a decision and never buy the first one you try just because it is the first one. It is seldom possible to have a horse on trial before purchase in today's economic climate, so try the horse really well when you go to see it. Take an experienced person with you and ask questions. Note the answers. Find out, preferably by doing it, what the horse is like to catch, groom, tack up, ride alone, ride in company, ride in the open, ride on the roads, school and jump. How does it behave in the stable and does it exhibit any stereotypies such as crib-biting, weaving or box walking? (These behaviours were commonly referred to in the past

as 'vices', a term which is scientifically incorrect and does the horse an injustice, see Chapter 2.) If necessary, go back and try the horse a second time before you make up your mind.

Experienced horse people say the most important thing about buying a horse is that you must like it: 'I wouldn't buy one that I wouldn't want to look at made of china on the mantelpiece,' said one. This is a good reference for your first impression, but then you must look much deeper and never buy a horse only because you like it. Like the pretty but fiery chestnut mare bought by a nervous, highly strung, red-haired lady acquaintance of ours, it may be quite unsuitable! She had a vision of riding her horse, mane and tail flying in the wind, cantering over the moors, with the horse amenable to her every wish. In reality, the little mare had a mind of her own and although perfectly amenable to a firm, calm rider with a good seat, her independent spirit frightened her novice owner, who would have done much better with a sensible cob.

An all-round family cob.

Chapter 2

Basic Handling and Safety on the Ground

Inevitably, more time is spent handling the horse on the ground than riding it and this is where problems begin. If you grow up around animals, respect for their behaviour becomes second nature; if not, you have to learn from scratch.

It was ingrained in us as children not to approach a horse from behind, never to make a sudden, unexpected move, to offer food on the flat of your palm and to handle the legs from the side, not the front or back. Now we will look at ways to carry out basic tasks safely from the ground, and in such a way that the horse accepts and understands them.

Safety

First, let us think about the handler. It is a hot day and you are out in sandals, shorts and T-shirt when you suddenly remember you meant to bring the horse in. You cannot be bothered to fetch a headcollar so you put a piece of string around the horse's neck and start to lead it in when a bird flies out of a bush. The horse leaps sideways, lands on your bare foot and pulls the string from your ungloved hand. As you hop about, nursing your burned hand and crushed toes, your unrepentant horse disappears into the distance.

The moral of this story is, do not be paranoid, but never take unnecessary chances either. The horse is a large animal and much stronger than you are. Accidents that happen may not be its fault, but may have just as unpleasant results.

Even experienced people sometimes take unnecessary risks. Ninety-nine times out of a hundred, we get away with it because we are aware of what we do and reduce the risk to the minimum. The one hundredth time, when we are momentarily distracted, or have not anticipated or allowed sufficiently for the horse's unpredictability, an accident happens.

For example, two of us went to catch a mare that was preventing a stallion from covering another mare in the same field. I caught the stallion first, as it is not sensible to remove a mare from a loose stallion. To fasten his headcollar, I briefly turned away from the mares. In those few moments, the dominant mare dashed in and lashed out at the stallion. Her flying hoof connected just above my knee, shattering my femur. A few moments of concentration on one thing at the expense of another and the result was eight months out of action.

In retrospect, it is easy to say that I should have kept my eye on the mare. In practice, however, it is impossible to eliminate risk entirely from our relationship with these powerful, volatile animals, and we can only do our best to minimise it.

Clothing

The staff at any well-run equestrian yard should wear a basic uniform of safe clothing. Despite all arguments to the contrary, it is a wise precaution to wear approved safety headgear as much when on the ground as when riding, even when handling older, basically sensible horses. A startled horse's hoof flying past your ear is sufficient warning of the need to do this. Keep a helmet hanging with the headcollars and you will remember to wear it.

Sleeves, even short or rolled up, minimise skin damage and bruises from nips or head rubbing, while gloves are essential for leading or any form of in-hand training in order to protect your hands from rope burns. They also give a much better grip when necessary.

Jodhpurs are comfortable and practical for work both on and off the horse, while hard-wearing denim jeans or moleskins are suitable if working mostly on the ground. Suede or leather full chaps are warm in winter and protect your clothes whilst allowing you freedom of movement. For riding, half chaps and short boots are comfortable and, provided the boots have ankle support, give more flexibility and freedom of movement than long rubber riding boots.

There are many alternatives on the market, from inexpensive 'riding trainers' with a heel, to purpose-engineered riding boots. They must have a heel of at least 13 mm (0.5 in) to avoid the risk of slipping through the stirrup iron. Toe protection is advisable and ankle support is essential for long-term wear. You should be able to trust your boots enough to move fast in them without the risk of tripping, having them slip at the heel, or being pulled off by a horse stepping on your heel.

Do not feel that you are getting unnecessarily 'dressed up' in this gear. Treat it as normal wear whenever you are dealing with your horse and it will soon feel natural and right.

Your position around the horse

Watch two horses meeting for the first time and you will see that they approach each other obliquely, nose towards shoulder. This approach indicates forbearance and caution, coupled with curiosity. They want to investigate one another, but are each aware that the other could be more dominant.

Neither wants to start an argument it could lose, so they approach in a way that signifies no threat. At the same time, they may give signals warning the other horse to be cautious too, such as arching the neck and stepping high, flaring the nostrils, lifting the tail and snorting to make themselves look bigger and more intimidating. They approach slowly, ready to leap away from the other if threatened.

What happens next depends on the signals they receive from each other. A very young horse, for example will 'mouth' or 'snap' at an elder, with neck outstretched and head lowered as a sign of submission. Horses that know each other may simply touch noses and wander off companionably. Strangers may circle away and back and exhibit a variety of snorts, nickers and squeals, sniffing all over, striking out, chasing, running away and returning before they decide which is the dominant party and settle down.

As a human approaching a horse, first you need to establish that you are no threat and, second, that you are the dominant party in the relationship. If you walk straight up to a horse's head, looking it in the eye, with your body square to their body, it will

This is a stand-off. The mare on the left has been newly introduced to the field and after some galloping around, the others have decided to ignore her.

Curiosity gets the better of Ria and she approaches Kashala. Kashala, the stranger, keeps her head submissively lowered.

Ria gives Kashala a thorough investigation.

Finally, nose to nose contact is made and Kashala is accepted.

perceive you as a threat. This is how a predator approaches, once the element of surprise is lost. Even a trained horse, accustomed to humans, may lift his head and regard you warily if you approach in this way.

Therefore, approach any horse as another horse would, obliquely and to the shoulder, without looking the horse in the eye. Make contact by stroking the shoulder, then the neck and let the horse make contact with you by smelling you. Your touch should be smooth and positive, neither tickling nor invasive. If you show nervousness, the horse will take this as a form of uncertainty and may question your authority with a small challenge, such as moving away or raising its head if you try to put on its headcollar. The most experienced and best-trained horse will play games with its handler if invited to do so.

However, if you are quietly positive, a trained horse should adopt the subservient role and accept you. A lowered head shows that the horse is relaxed and accepts you, so you can proceed with whatever you want to do. A raised head denotes tension and wariness.

When you first meet a horse, try to spend some time getting to know it before you ride. If possible, tack it up yourself, although some riding schools insist on doing it for you. In this case at least give the horse a few moments to reassure itself about you on the ground, otherwise how can it be expected to accept you confidently on its back? If the riding school disapproves, find a new one! Nothing to do with horses should ever be hurried.

When moving around a horse, always make sure it knows where you are. Remember there is a blind spot to the rear, so if you want to change sides behind the horse, run your hand over its quarters to let it know you are there. Touching the horse like this gives it a chance to connect your body, in a physical sense, with what you are doing to it. If you want to pick up a foot, run your hand down the leg so the horse anticipates your request and is not startled. Finally, keep yourself out of danger's way. This definitely does not mean at arm's length. Arm's length is ideal kicking distance!

Once a horse accepts you in its personal space, get in close. If you are relaxed and working close to the horse's body, it will have confidence in you. If you are fiddling about nervously at arm's length,

the horse will sense your unease and be tense and ready for 'flight or fight' at the least provocation. Horses huddle close together for reassurance and they accept a human in this role as readily as another horse. The risk of being kicked will be minimised if you place yourself a) out of the line of fire and b) where a kick is least likely to do damage, that is, either so close that it has not gained momentum, or completely out of range.

A powerful, punching kick with the hind legs is the most dangerous type of kick possible and usually occurs if the horse is startled from behind. So far as the horse knows, the thing behind it could easily be a lion! Horses get kicked in this way by other horses when they are ridden too close too quickly, especially if they are strangers, but sometimes even when they know each other well. The horse in front is alarmed by the sudden, uninvited invasion of its space and so lashes out to protect itself, sometimes with tragic results. Never ride close behind another horse without due warning and make sure the horse in front can see you and is happy about your approach. If it flattens its ears and threatens to kick, stay back, or leave a wide space as you pass.

Horses also cow kick, a sideways kick that may occur when something is irritating them, such as having their tummy brushed too vigorously, or a fly

Tony is spending time with the new foals and Rafiki is intrigued. Rosy, an experienced brood mare, knows that Tony is no threat and the position of her ears shows that she is not particularly worried. Nevertheless, she comes purposefully to check on her offspring.

There is no doubt what Tara's body language is saying, and the foal is rapidly turned away.

The same horse with a dominant human. She is investigating Tony's moustache with her lips and her expression and the position of the ears show that there is no threat offered here. However, we do not advise you to try this!

A youngster 'mouthing' in submission as he greets an older sibling.

Baby Rose's lowered head and relaxed jaw shows complete trust and submission.

Ria lets Merlin know that she will kick if he comes any closer. Her head is down and her back rounded, ready to lash out.

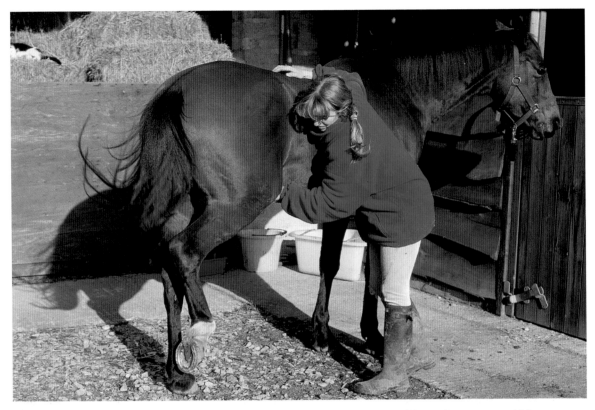

Becky's brush is tickling and Tammy swishes her tail in warning and lifts her hind leg to threaten a cow kick.

The double-barrelled backward kick is the most dangerous, but the colt has learned to keep out of the way of real harm. Humans are often slower at getting out of the way.

buzzing around. A sensitive horse may cow kick if the girth is done up too roughly. This type of kick does not usually carry a great deal of force, but can still give you a nasty bruise.

Forward striking with the hooves is a sign that a horse is angry, frightened and defensive, or giving warning about something. It is part of the stallion's repertoire of fighting moves. Mares may do it when meeting stallions or other horses. Striking out, especially combined with a rear, is very dangerous and can inflict a nasty injury. A horse that does it must be immediately and strongly reprimanded. Fortunately, it is a habit that mostly occurs in boisterous, young horses and they soon give it up with correct training.

Catching and leading

A horse's acceptance of being led depends upon how well it was taught as a youngster (see Chapters 9 and 11). A headcollar is sufficient most of the time, although a controller halter is useful for training and there are several designs available. Occasionally, an in-hand bridle or a chifney may be appropriate. A chifney is a bit designed to prevent rearing, usually used for stallions.

Some horses canter up as you enter their field, others are wilier. All you need do with the former is walk quietly to the shoulder and slip the headcollar under the throat, over the nose and the long end over the poll to fasten on the near side.

If a horse is difficult to catch, ask yourself why. Is it afraid or unhappy about what happens once it is caught? Or is it just playing games? We knew a pony that could be caught easily by anyone except the owner. Why? The owner lacked confidence and was nervous. The pony knew it and took advantage. It is essential to believe in your own ability to handle your horse. This self-confidence and belief is communicated to the horse via your body language and, in most cases, is all the persuasion the horse needs.

Sometimes, horses make a game of being caught. Ours occasionally do this and instead of coming to call will trot, or even gallop in circles around the field with their tails in the air. You can tell it is a game by the way they keep one eye on you as they prance around. 'Come and get me,' they seem to be saying and if you try, off they go again. If you stand

still and pretend to be interested in something else, they soon realise you are not going to play and either stand in a corner and wait for you, or come to see what it is that is fascinating you so much.

The horse that genuinely does not want to be caught is a different matter. There is always a reason: either the horse connects being caught with some consequence that it dislikes, for example leaving its friends or its grass, or it has had some bad experiences after being caught in the past, for example insensitive or rough treatment in previous ownership.

We bought a mare that was difficult to catch, due to past rough treatment. Initially, a bowl of feed was needed to tempt her. I made a great fuss of her and made sure that we only did things she enjoyed – gentle grooming and massage – until she began to recover her confidence in people. It was several months before she would trust my husband to catch her but eventually she was as easy to catch as any of our homebred horses.

If your horse really does not want to be caught and makes for the far end of the field with obvious determination, its ears back, tail clamped down and gaze averted, there has to be a reason such as this. Is it your treatment that it dislikes, or something that happened in the past? Whatever the reason, you need to show it that being caught has pleasant results. A horse should enjoy its work. If it does not, there is something wrong with your attitude or your methods. Find the reason and you can solve the catching problem. Make a point of visiting the field when you do not want to catch the horse for work. Talk to it and encourage it to look forwards to seeing you – frequent titbits are not advisable although the odd treat does no harm.

If the horse will come close enough to snatch a titbit but dashes away before you get the headcollar on, try the following technique. Keep the headcollar and rope tucked down over your arm as you approach. Hold out your hand with the titbit or, if necessary, a bucket with some food. With a bucket, wait for the horse to put its head well into it, then slip the leadrope around its neck and hold it just below the jaw. As far as the horse is concerned, it is now caught. With the rope around its poll and held under the jaw, you have more control than with it further down the neck, making it more difficult to pull away. Put the headcollar on without releasing the leadrope. If you have a titbit, do not allow the horse to take it until you have slipped the leadrope around its neck. Whether you need a titbit or a bucket will depend upon how determined the horse is to avoid being caught. Once you have caught your horse, do not always ride. Lead the horse around the field a couple of times, make a fuss of it and let it go. The idea is to break the association of being caught with an unpleasant consequence. When the horse no longer connects the two things, catching will cease to be a problem.

Leading

A well-trained horse walks quietly beside you with the leadrope slack. Traditional management states that the handler should walk beside the horse's shoulder; however, we find that it is more practical to be slightly further forwards, especially when handling young horses. You have more options for control if the horse suddenly spooks and it is less easy for the horse to leap ahead of you and pull away. Hold the leadrope about 30 cm (1 ft) from the horse's head in your nearest hand with the slack in your other hand. Never wrap the rope around your hand. If the horse pulls away you will get a nasty rope burn or even crushed fingers and, should the horse panic, you could be pulled over if your hand is tangled in the rope. If the slack is long, either coil it in large loops, or back and forth.

When leading, look ahead to where you are going, not at the horse. This will give the horse confidence, whereas if you look at him, he is more likely to stop, or balk, or be reluctant. The horse should walk along freely with you, not rushing ahead, dragging back, or pushing against you. Many young horses, lacking in confidence, do the latter for the reassurance of touch. Some never grow out of it and need to be re-trained. A schooled horse can be led quietly in a headcollar and without need of a whip. For more on teaching a horse to lead see Chapter 11.

A chifney bit attached to a simple headstall is useful for horses inclined to rear or be excitable. Otherwise, it is not advisable to lead from the bit, as you risk putting strong pressure on the mouth – the very part you want to be sensitive to your aids when ridden. The 'be nice' halter, which tightens on the horse's head if it pulls, is a very useful alternative, and is one of the controller halters mentioned above.

Tying up

All mature riding horses should have been trained to stand quietly when tied up. Ideally, a tied horse should never be left unattended although it is bound to happen sometimes – when you have forgotten your gloves, or the phone is ringing, for instance. Therefore, it is essential to ensure that the horse is

There is an art to catching and leading. Baby Rose is walking too fast and getting ahead, putting tension on the halter. This 'be nice' halter will tighten on her head until she releases the pressure herself by slowing down.

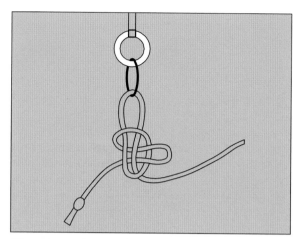

The more usual one as above.

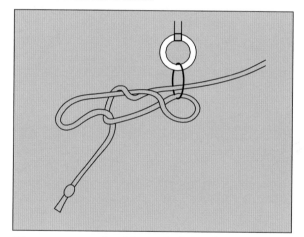

However, we prefer this method, it releases the rope completely when pulled.

tied safely and in such a way that if it is startled, the tie will break without risk of the horse becoming hung up or injured. Horses have died as a result of unsafe tying up.

First, be sure that the building, fence, or rail to which the horse is tied is secure and immovable. Never tie a horse to a gate that does not have a reversed top hinge, as a startled horse is easily capable of jerking even a heavy five-bar gate off its hinges. A horse galloping off, terrified, with a large gate in tow is a situation likely to end in disaster. Second, never tie a horse directly to a rail, fence or tie-ring. Attach a length of string, then tie the leadrope to the string. If the horse jerks back, the string will break with reasonable ease, avoiding

injury to the horse and damage to your headcollar or rope. Modern bale twine is often used, but is strong when new and the leadrope may break instead, so use an alternative, or split the string. Third, use a quick release knot so that the horse can be untied by a single pull on the end of the rope if necessary.

There are two methods.

If a horse resents being tied and habitually pulls back or refuses to stand quietly, it should be re-trained as for a young horse (see Chapter 11).

In the stable

Most horses are not terribly keen on being shut inside. To a horse, whose safety lies in the ability to run from danger, the stable represents dangerous confinement, so it is hardly surprising that its natural inclination is to come out as soon as the door is opened. However, a horse that grows up sharing a stable at first with its mother, then with or adjoining friends or siblings learns that this small, rather dark area can be a pleasant place after all, especially in a cold, wet winter. Entering the stable can become associated with pleasant experiences such as being fed, groomed or massaged, and with human companionship. Horses vary in their attitude towards the stable. Some never become completely comfortable inside, while others, given the option to wander in and out, spend as much time in as out.

Once inside, the horse must learn to stand back, move over, refrain from biting or kicking and accept being handled and groomed. Trouble often begins because a youngster stabled alone for the first time is not taught good manners from the beginning (see Chapter 11). Good manners are an abstract concept, which the horse cannot understand. However, it can learn to respond to various consistent signals given by the handler. The principles outlined in the previous chapter are all that are needed to teach good stable manners. The horse must learn to associate a signal (e.g., pressure on the chest) with a response (e.g., a step back) in return for which it gets an immediate reward (e.g., praise and rubbing of the body area that made the response). The reward reinforces the response so that the horse is more inclined to make the correct response next time. The few seconds it takes each time to encourage the horse to behave acceptably in the stable are well worth the effort. A horse which tries to barge out when you walk in with the saddle, or to thrust its head in the feed bucket, or worse, threatens to bite or kick when you take in its feed, is an irritation at best and can spoil your pleasure in ownership at worst.

The horse's natural inclination to respond to pressure with pressure has been well researched and documented. The handler's job is to persuade the horse to move away from pressure and this is done by showing the horse that moving into pressure causes it discomfort. In his book, *Natural Horsemanship,* American trainer Pat Parelli explains that steady pressure that increases if the horse does not respond as required is more effective than a momentary jabbing or poking pressure. If you poke at a horse on a sensitive spot, it may well be startled into reacting by moving, though not necessarily in the direction you would like. If you poke an insensitive spot, it may ignore you altogether. However, steady pressure gives the horse time to work out that if it moves in a direction opposite to the pressure, the pressure and discomfort is relieved. This response is then reinforced by a) the pressure immediately being discontinued and b) the reward of praise and rubbing the appropriate spot. Next time the horse will respond more quickly.

If gentle persuasion has no effect, the handler may need to use increasing pressure and be firmly dominant to overcome ingrained bad manners. Light, fingertip pressure becomes deeper and stronger. Each measure used is a stronger version of the previous one. Immediately the horse makes a move, even if only to lift a leg in the right direction, it should be rewarded with praise and rubbing of the area where you introduced the pressure. Things that will not work include inconsistent pushing on different parts of the body, and a high-pitched or whining use of the voice. Where voice aids are appropriate, the tone should be consistent and firm. Smacking the horse's chest is ineffectual, while hitting his face will make him head-shy and both will hurt your hand.

The horse should move over in response to the voice command, coupled with a light nudge at the girth where you would use your leg. If the horse does not understand this, apply light pressure, increasing it until the horse responds, in conjunction with a firm 'Over' from your voice. Do not forget the immediate reward of stroking and praise. Eventually, a horse will anticipate the command whenever you raise your hand to his side and click your tongue.

Always rewarding your horse for a good response will ensure that it remembers a lesson. Rubbing and stroking make the horse feel good and it will often lower its head, indicating a calm and relaxed state of mind. Hearty slaps on the neck, or even strong 'pats' are not appreciated. They startle and unnerve the horse, usually causing it to throw its head up, step away, or roll its eye, showing the white sclera. At best, the horse may stiffen its neck and tighten its lips in dislike.

If you want to put a greedy or over enthusiastic horse's feed in its manger without being trampled on or crushed, do not try to creep around it. Keep the bucket away from its nose and face up to it squarely, growling at it to stand back. This is the pose of a threatening predator, of whom the horse should be wary. Flick your fingers at it, or use chest pressure if you can do so safely. When teaching this kind of lesson it is important not to overdo it, or become excitable yourself. You want the horse to learn the acceptable limits of behaviour, not terrify it into becoming a cowed, nervous beast.

As soon as the horse shows the slightest response, by raising its head and taking one step back, stop threatening it and reward it. Only threaten again if it repeats the barging. Provided you are firm, consistent and determined, the horse will soon learn what it may and may not do in the stable.

Behavioural stereotypies/stable 'vices'

So-called stable vices – crib biting, wind sucking, weaving and box walking – are now more appropriately referred to as behavioural stereotypies. They are related to the horse's discomfort at some perceived cause for anxiety.

We noticed a young gelding begin to crib bite when he was brought in for his early education and training. He was being asked to accept and learn new things and although he knew and trusted his handler, he was restless and uncertain what was going on when he was being groomed, asked to pick up his feet and then tacked up. Grabbing hold of the top of the stable door seemed to be a displacement activity in which he indulged to distract himself from his restlessness. We solved the tendency by moving him

A collar used to discourage crib biting – it may treat the symptom, but does not solve the cause.

Anti-weaving grille.

quietly away from the source of temptation, turning him around, or taking him outside and generally distracting his attention from the habit. The phase soon passed, but why did he do it?

Most horses develop these habits when unattended, in response to distress at being denied their natural pattern of behaviour. They occur more frequently in horses that are stabled for most of their time. It has been established that endorphins – natural opiates produced in the body – are released

33

in response to stress and it appears that they, in turn, trigger a chemical response in the nerve cells which causes repetitive behaviour patterns, stereotyped upon the horse's most natural basic functions, that is, eating and moving.

In the case of our youngster, the new things that were happening to him caused him a certain amount of stress – a normal response in an intelligent animal. This triggered the release of endorphins, which then stimulated a desire for action. There was nothing to eat and nowhere for him to go, so he diverted his desire into an abnormal replacement activity – that of crib biting.

In addition to heightening the desire to continue natural behaviours, the release of endorphins has a pain-killing effect, so a horse will continue the abnormal replacement behaviours it learns to the extent of damaging itself.

Put simply, the imposition of mental stress causes a physical stimulus that requires a response of normal action. When a natural physical reaction is denied, an abnormal one based on a normal one takes its place.

Crib biting and wind sucking

These are stereotypies based on eating; wind sucking being a form of the behaviour carried out without the need for a surface to grasp. From a practical point of view the habits may not prevent the horse being used for riding, unless they result in loss of condition or colic. Tooth wear in the crib-biter is a practical consideration that will cause difficulties in eating later in life once the incisors become excessively worn down. Physical methods of prevention, such as fitting a 'cribbing collar' or treating or adapting the stable surfaces so as to make gripping them with the teeth impossible, may minimise the results of crib biting. However, they do not remove the cause and can morally be considered neither a cure nor an acceptable recourse for a dedicated horse handler.

Ideally, the reasons for a horse crib biting need to be analysed and overcome as soon as the habit is noticed as, unfortunately, it can become so ingrained that it may continue even when the primary cause is removed, that is, when the horse is turned out instead of being stabled.

Weaving and box walking

These stereotypies are based on the horse's need for constant movement, as when grazing or moving from place to place. Keeping moving within the herd is part of the natural defence system of the grazing animal. If you stop, you are more likely to be singled out and caught by a predator.

Weaving tends to occur in the restless horse that is confined for long hours with nothing to do. Once the haynet is empty, the horse seeks another outlet for its energy and, finding none, begins to shift alternately from one forefoot to the other – an abnormal response to a stimulus for normal action. This horse needs to be turned out for longer and be given more work of a more varied nature, so that it reverts to spending its time in the stable resting and eating. Stable 'toys', such as a horse-ball or a tyre or turnip suspended from the ceiling, may help for periods when stabling cannot be avoided.

A V-shaped grille placed over the door is a common sight, but may just result in the horse weaving behind the grille. Full height grilles, which confirm the horse's isolation by preventing even visual contact with neighbours, are most unkind and are likely to increase the incidence of weaving. They are most often seen in stallion boxes.

Box walking occurs most frequently in the super-fit, athletic horse that is temporarily confined, especially in a strange place, for example, at an event. It may also happen with inexperienced or nervous animal confined for the first time, or due to injury or illness, or in any horse suffering a high level of stress coupled with confinement. Again, it is an abnormal response to the stress stimulus requiring the normal response of movement. The solution is to remove the cause, for example, by making sure horses have an opportunity to work, or graze and relax before stabling after a journey, or corralling outside instead of stabling. The most difficult situation is where injury to a foot or leg requires box rest and the horse is too fit to rest quietly, so walks the box incessantly. We resolved one such case by putting up a small 'stable-sized' outdoor corral with electric fencing and moving it each day. The horse was confined, but gave up box walking because it relaxed once it was outdoors and could see its friends and surroundings.

Chapter 3

Handling the Horse for Grooming and Routine Treatments

A well-trained horse that is comfortable in human company will often happily stand untied for grooming, but if you are in doubt, it is safest to tie it up. We teach all our youngsters to accept being tied, but then frequently handle them untied in the stable. They appreciate the freedom to raise, lower and turn their heads and are better able to communicate with the handler when untied. Horses are curious; they like to see and smell what is going on and will often follow you around the stable, or pick up items of grooming kit, as well as watch what you are doing.

If a horse is enjoying the sensation of being groomed, it may even lower its head and doze, which it cannot do if tied up short. Alternatively, the horse may indulge in mutual grooming with a human as it does with another horse, scratching your back with its teeth in response to the stimulation of the brush. Horses use surprisingly strong pressure when doing this so make sure you are wearing enough protective clothing over vulnerable areas! Be pleased if your horse exhibits this trusting behaviour and do not reprimand it, even though it may not be as pleasurable for you as for another horse.

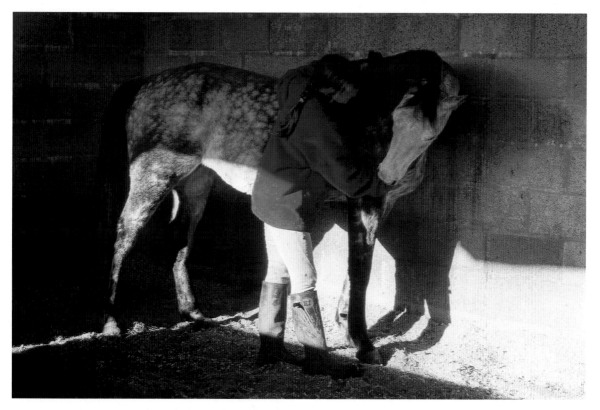

Tara enjoys some 'hands on' treatment from Becky. Given the opportunity, horses will often turn their heads to see what you are doing, or to indulge in mutual grooming.

Grooming

Grooming has several purposes: it removes dirt, sweat, loose hair and skin debris from the coat and stimulates the circulation. It also makes the horse look attractive and gives you an opportunity to check closely for any minor injuries or other physical problems.

Horses react to grooming in various ways. The thinner and more sensitive the skin, the more careful you need to be. Some horses can take quite vigorous brushing, even with a stiff-bristled dandy brush. Others find even a soft-bristled body brush invasive. You cannot expect a horse to stand still and accept discomfort.

Basic grooming

For a grass-kept horse, brush over with a dandy brush to remove dried mud, gently remove tangles from the mane and tail with a softer brush, clean eyes and nose with a damp sponge, use a separate sponge for the dock and pick out the hooves. No more is necessary as the horse needs to retain the natural oils in its coat for weather protection. A stabled horse is usually also groomed thoroughly with a body brush, to remove scurf and stimulate the circulation.

Remember to begin by approaching the horse's shoulder and start with a few strokes there. If the horse is calm, you can move up to the top of the neck and work your way back to the quarters. Be aware that brushing over bony areas causes more discomfort than over muscled areas and temper your pressure accordingly. Keep your brush strokes smooth and firm. Avoid banging the brush down on the horse's body, pressing too hard, or using tentative little strokes that tickle. Be respectful. Avoid rubbing too vigorously at stubborn patches of mud. Sometimes an alternative tool, such as a rubber or plastic curry comb or a 'cactus cloth', will be more effective and acceptable to the horse than the bristles of a dandy brush, particularly if it has a thin coat and sensitive skin.

Some horses are especially sensitive under the belly, so be particularly gentle. Also take care not to knock the legs, which have bones just under the skin, unprotected by muscles. When moving around

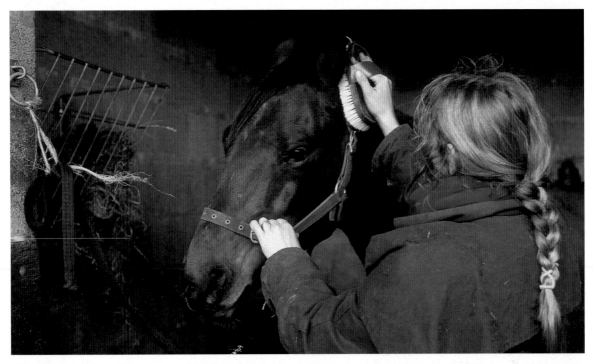

Tammy accepts the soft brush around her ears, but there is just enough tension in her muzzle and general expression to let the handler know she isn't enjoying this much.

Horses are infinitely curious. Tammy is a grown up horse, but Becky still shows her the milk crate she is going to stand on to pull her mane.

If a horse dislikes having its mane pulled, the job is often easier if you pull the hairs straight upwards, rather than down.

the horse, remember the safety rules explained in Chapter 2 – stay close to the horse's body, make no sudden moves and avoid waving grooming implements around in front of the horse's face.

Some horses dislike having their manes and tails groomed. Tangles must be removed without breaking the hairs and this can be difficult with a brush. Badly tangled hair is best separated using your fingers. When grooming manes and tails, begin at the hair ends and work your way up to the roots. By working this way less hair is pulled out and the process is more comfortable for the horse.

To pick out a horse's foot, you first have to persuade the horse to lift the foot and consent to the foot being held. This is a very unnatural thing for a horse to accept as it depends upon the absolute freedom of its feet and legs to flee from danger at an instant's notice. Man has influenced only a tiny period in the evolution of the horse, but it is perhaps a measure of how greatly the equine has come to trust and depend upon humans that it allows us to restrain it in a way that so strongly contradicts its natural inclinations.

To pick out a forefoot, stand close to the horse's side, facing its tail, bend and run the hand nearest the body down the horse's leg. Some horses will lift the leg in response to a tug on the fetlock hair, others to finger and thumb pressure on the tendon on either side above the fetlock and still others in anticipatory response to your touch and the command 'Pick up'. If a horse is stubborn, you can persuade it to shift its weight to the opposite leg by leaning against its shoulder. It then becomes possible to lift the nearer leg. Some people think this is the wrong solution as the horse may then lean its weight on the handler. We have never had this problem and once the horse has learned that it must rebalance itself in order to pick up a particular foot, it does so with increasing ease and willingness.

Some horses snatch the foot back down as soon as it is picked up. This can be overcome by holding the foot up lightly, at the toe only, with your fingertips. Provided you keep your fingers in place, with the foot flexed, the horse can then neither lean on you nor get enough weight into it to put it down straight.

Pick the hoof out cleanly, using the hoofpick away from the heels towards the toe. This avoids any risk of the hoofpick digging into the more sensitive areas of the foot. At the same time, check the shoes for wear and the clenches for security. Follow the same procedure for the hind feet, again standing close beside the horse, facing the tail.

Presentation and turnout

Pulling manes and tails

Most horses have their manes pulled for neatness and to enable plaiting, even if not subjected to other methods of beautification! Some stand like donkeys, others make considerable fuss. So how do you pull a mane without trauma?

First, hair comes out more easily if the horse is warmed up, so, ideally, save mane pulling until after exercise. Second, try to do the job regularly, so that you avoid having to do too much at once. If you do have a long mane to pull, do it in several short sessions, so the horse does not have to stand still for too long, and justifiably become fed up and irritable.

You will need something convenient to stand on, such as a milk crate. Even a small horse can stretch up beyond comfortable reach. If you do not know the horse well, give it a minute or two to get used to your sudden increase in height before starting to pull the mane.

Mane pulling can be done with the fingers only, although this is hard on your hands. There are also special tools available which comb and cut the hair, in theory making the job easier, but the most common method is to use a short-toothed metal comb.

- **Start towards the withers. The hair usually comes out more easily there and the horse will be less agitated than if you begin at the poll.**
- **Comb the hair down, then back-comb so that only a few hairs remain taut in the comb, held between your forefinger and thumb.**
- **Wind these around the comb once or twice and give a sharp tug.**
- **Discard the loose hair and comb the mane straight again. With practice this procedure can be repeated rapidly.**
- **Work your way up the neck to the poll.**

If the horse becomes irritable, take fewer hairs each time, or take a break and do something else for a few minutes.

Giving a haynet is not a good idea as the horse will move its head around too much for you to concentrate on accurate pulling. Sometimes pulling the hairs out in an upward direction, in line with the way the hair grows as opposed to downward, can be helpful. When working on an unpulled mane, avoid shortening it too much until you see how it falls, or you may end up with a 'punk' style hairdo! Pulling both shortens and thins the mane and experience will show the right amount for your horse.

Tails are pulled in much the same way, the hairs being pulled from the sides of the dock so that the tail lies neatly between the quarters instead of spreading out over them. The important thing is to avoid being kicked, so you should work from each side alternately and not stand directly behind the horse. If a horse is an unknown quantity, or known to be fractious, it is a good idea to have a solid barrier between it and yourself, such as a stable door. Tails can be plaited instead of pulled and we prefer this, because the horses retain the full protection of their tail hair against bad weather and flies. We avoid pulling manes shorter than necessary for the same reason.

Trimming

This entails the removal of excess hair from various areas to make the horse look neater. For safety's sake, as horses often move quickly and unpredictably, blunt-ended scissors or special trimming clippers should be used. We trim a very narrow bridlepath behind the ears at the poll, so that the bridle can sit comfortably without a bunch of hair underneath. If necessary, we trim the mane at the withers to avoid it being caught under the saddle, or rubbed and broken by the breastplate. Tails are also banged off square (i.e. cut straight across), 15 cm (6 in) below the hock. This is adequate for normal riding, but for showing, you

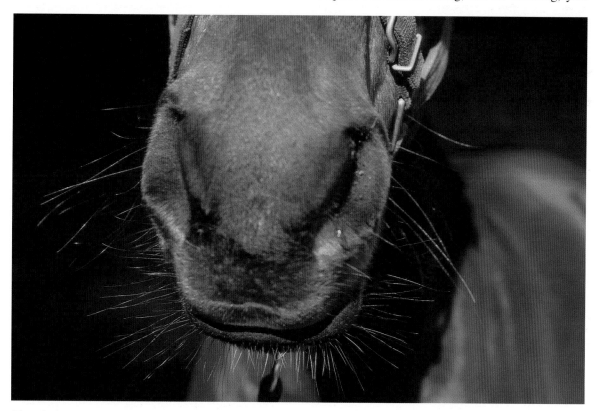

The whiskers are used for sensory purposes.

Before starting to clip, hold the clippers flat against the horse's shoulder with the motor running, to accustom her to the noise and vibration.

Begin clipping at the shoulder. The horse has her ears backwards to listen to the clippers.

may want to do a little more.

Hairy fetlocks can be trimmed neatly to follow the line of the leg and remove the 'feather', though we prefer to leave them untrimmed, again for protection in wet weather. Native pony and heavy horse breeds should be left untrimmed in any case.

The edges of the ears can be tidied, if you really must, by holding them together and trimming any protruding hair. However, the hair inside the ears should be left well alone as it protects the delicate inner structures from flies and the ingress of any other unwanted debris, as well as bad weather.

The whiskers are a sensory organ and, fortunately, even the showing fraternity mostly now accept that their removal is both unkind and unnecessary.

Clipping

The main reason for clipping the horse's coat is to enable it to work during the winter without undue sweating. A sweat-drenched winter coat quickly

becomes cold when the horse stops moving and increases the risk of a cold or chill. Obviously, suitable rugs are needed to keep the clipped horse warm when it is not working.

Clipping is carried out in various patterns to suit the amount and type of work being done and the handler's preference as to design! A neck and belly clip may be given to horses in light work and is most often used for natives and other ponies, which can then be left un-rugged except in severe weather. A trace clip can be done at varying heights: low if the horse is in light work and higher if the horse is working harder. These are frequently seen on the pleasure horse – ridden at weekends and occasionally during the week, turned out in a New Zealand rug during the day and brought in at night. The hair is removed from the lower half of the neck and body, along a horizontal plane from mid-shoulder to buttocks, with a semi-circle following the line of hair growth above the stifle. A blanket clip is similar except that all the neck hair is removed leaving a 'blanket'-shaped area over the back and quarters.

A chaser clip, which we normally use, is the type often given to National Hunt racehorses. The hair is removed below a sweeping line down the neck and body from behind the ear to the stifle. The hair is also removed from the lower half of the head, following the bridle line from behind the ear to above the corner of the mouth. We like this clip as it removes the hair from the areas most prone to sweating and mud splashes, but leaves the hind quarters fully protected and the horse can be turned out for an hour or two without a rug on fine days. In all these clips the leg hair is left on, for warmth and protection against injury.

The hunter clip is more extensive and is intended for fully stabled horses in hard work. The coat is clipped out with the exception of the saddle patch, which helps protect the back from sores, and the legs. A full clip removes the hair also from the saddle patch and legs and is really only suitable for showjumpers competing indoors, where the atmosphere can be very warm at a big show.

Clipping a horse is one job you should not undertake alone without first gaining some practical advice and help from an experienced person. You need to watch it done and then try it yourself on a quiet horse under supervision before attempting to clip your own horse. The safety rules must be meticulously observed to avoid the risk of an accident or electric shock. We find that cordless clippers that have their own rechargeable power pack are most convenient to use. There is no long lead to the mains to worry about and the clippers can be used anywhere.

To clip successfully, you need good, preferably natural light on a dry day with no wind. The horse must be clean and dry – do not attempt to clip a sweaty, dirty, matted or damp coat, or you will blunt the blades and may easily injure the horse. The clip pattern can be marked out with chalk or clipped by eye, if you have a good eye for form. A chaser clip, which involves only one continuous line, is the easiest design for beginners.

You need a clear floor area, so the clippings can be swept up easily and the horse should be tied up safely and fairly short. A haynet may help keep a fidgety horse quiet, but you will have to remove it to clip the head and neck and the job is easier if you can avoid giving one.

Older horses, which have been clipped many times before, should know what it is all about and stand quietly. A few horses are genuinely frightened and never bring themselves to accept the sound and feel of the clippers. These are best sedated by the vet and clipped by an experienced person – there is no point in risking injury if the horse reacts dangerously. You can tell if a horse is really frightened or just messing about by the look in its eyes and general demeanour as well as the degree of violence of its behaviour.

Many horses being clipped for the first time accept it with no fuss; others use it as an excuse to exert a challenge. Switch the clippers on, making sure the tension is correct, and stand close to the horse for a few moments. Next, place your free hand on the horse's shoulder so that it can feel the vibration through your body. If all is well, rest the clippers against the horse's shoulder so it can get used to the feel of them. Finally, take a few short, firm strokes to remove hair from the shoulder. If there is no reaction, you can continue clipping. Clip strokes should be carried out with even pressure and a long, sweeping, steady movement, removing as much hair as possible at each stroke. This will help to create a smooth finish, with the minimum of ridges. Avoid going back over the same areas too many times, or you may abrade the skin and cause soreness or a rash.

From the shoulder you can work backwards, leaving the neck until last, or forwards and leave the hind end until last. We find that it is more difficult to clip the head and neck once the horse starts to become bored and restless and so prefer to clip the front first, provided the horse is quiet. Some horses have particular ticklish areas, so be prepared for a sudden reaction at any time. Oddly enough, most horses do not seem to mind having their tummies clipped. Take particular care over the bony areas and if the skin is too loose in difficult spots, hold it firm with your free hand. It is easier to do inside the elbow if a helper raises the foreleg for you.

If the horse is not frightened, but decides to play up, the only effective ploy is patience. If necessary, with a horse being clipped for the first time, do the job over several days. Young horses, in particular, have a low boredom threshold and it is pointless to

41

initiate a struggle by insisting on finishing a clip on a youngster which has behaved well for an acceptable period. Leave it and come back tomorrow.

Sometimes a horse will accept being clipped everywhere except for the top of the neck and the head, disliking the clipper noise close to the ears. We had a mare which reacted like this. She was not frightened but simply did not want to submit and in the process of jerking her head up and back, broke several tie strings. As soon as she was free, she stood looking defiant but quite calm. When I held the end of the leadrope, passed through the tie-ring, instead of tying it, she attempted to bite first me and then the clippers. Each time I tried to clip her neck, she jerked away.

I found a very simple solution. I just held the clippers (fortunately the cordless type) switched on against her coat. Wherever she went the clippers followed, just staying in place. After about five minutes, in which she learned that whatever she did she could not get away from the clippers, she gave up completely and stood quietly. By the time I was ready to clip her jawline, she was dozing, with her head drooping. Always remember that one advantage humans have over horses is superior powers of reason. Psychology will invariably win over brute force.

Handling the horse for others

Visits from various experts – farrier, vet, saddler – are routine in the riding horse's life and should take place with the minimum of fuss from the horse. The owner should also be calm. One of the reasons for this book is that Tony, who is a vet, spends much of his working life reassuring anxious owners and showing them how to handle their horses effectively and give prescribed treatment. It is quite astonishing how many owners tell him 'My horse won't let you inject him without a twitch,' or 'Be careful, he always bites (or kicks) the vet.' They are then amazed when he makes friends with the horse and carries out the required treatment with no more than token resistance.

The keys to Tony's success are:

- **Supreme self-confidence, which the horse can sense. This gives the horse confidence and establishes Tony's role as the leader.**
- **Patience, in allowing the horse time to analyse and accept his presence and smell.**
- **Calm determination in handling the horse, which includes frequent use of a deep, confident tone of voice, mostly to encourage, but also to reprimand if necessary.**

Tony's more nervous equine patients often end up with their head on his shoulder while he scratches their withers and talks nonsense to them. Only rarely will he resort to use of the twitch, for example on an injured horse that reacts violently to the prospect of repeated injections and may risk damaging itself further.

If you are lucky, your vet or farrier may have the patience and expertise to handle a difficult animal. However, that does not alter the fact that training the horse to behave is not the visiting expert's job and the work he has to do may be more difficult, or even impossible, if the horse is unmanageable. Too often, owners who do not bother to train their horses adequately, especially youngstock, think it will be quite all right to 'let the vet or farrier sort it out'. However, trimming and balancing a horse's foot, for example, is a skilled job in the best of circumstances. How can a farrier be expected to do a good job if the horse in question resents picking up its foot, then charges around the box on three legs, goes down on its knees, or up in the air and generally refuses to co-operate? Most farriers simply do not have the time, even if they have the patience, to cope with this sort of problem and could not be blamed for simply walking away from it.

Let us see how such situations can be avoided.

Working environment

The stall, stable or yard where your horse is treated needs to be clean, clear and safe. Do not expect the vet or farrier to deal with your horse in the middle of a muddy field, or in a field shelter fetlock deep in dung. Hanging on to an unco-operative animal in wet slippery conditions is a prelude to an accident and there is also the matter of hygiene to be considered. For shoeing, horses are best tied or held outside in a clean yard in good light. For veterinary treatment, a stable with clean bedding is preferable. Remove any tools, wheel barrows, feed bowls, etc. from the box and ensure that there are no potentially dangerous projections in the way.

Safety equipment

The average horse soon gets used to being shod – after all it occurs at least every six weeks. Any other kind of treatment, however, is likely to be less familiar, whether it is a routine vet's visit, physiotherapy, or saddle fitting. Therefore, equip yourself with safe clothing – an approved helmet, sensible non-slip footwear, long-sleeved top and gloves – and your horse with a headcollar and leadrope in good repair.

Anticipate any extra equipment that might be needed – bucket of cold water for the farrier, warm water for the vet, lunge line and tackle, etc., depending on the job in hand, and have it ready and waiting before you start doing anything with the horse.

Pre-preparation of the horse

Professional visits are easier if the horse has basic good stable manners. It is well worth while spending time with your horse on the ground,

getting it used to various 'treatments'. The strange things the vet does will not then cause anxiety. All owners should know their horses' normal vital signs and taking the heart-rate (pulse) and temperature should be an every day part of good management.

The pulse is taken with a stethoscope, which can be purchased inexpensively from vets or endurance riding equipment stockists. The normal range of the horse's heart rate at rest (i.e., before exercise or feeding) is between 36 and 42 beats per minute, although some horses, especially fit competition horses, may have a lower resting rate.

To take the heart-rate, the stethoscope is placed against the chest, just behind the left elbow. You should hear a regular 'lub-dup' sound, which constitutes one complete heart-beat. The horse needs to stand quietly, without eating, for this to be heard clearly. You can count over a whole minute, or over 30 seconds and double the result to obtain the beats per minute. Some horses are ticklish at first, but soon become accustomed to the stethoscope if you take the pulse every day.

Taking the temperature is another simple procedure, which will also warn you if your horse is off colour and perhaps starting a virus or other illness.

Taking the pulse.

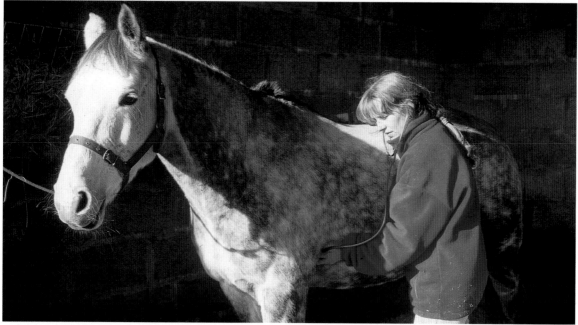

Taking the temperature.

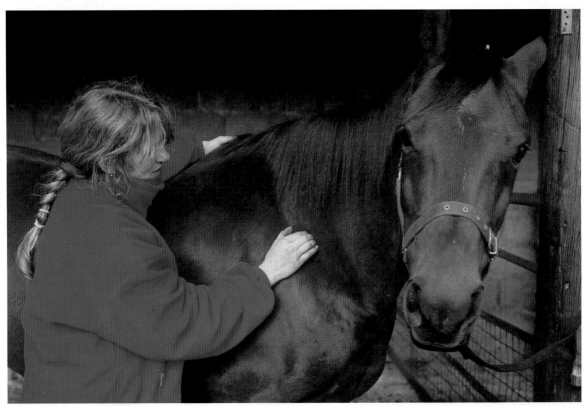

Massage is a good way to encourage horses to accept being handled all over.

- Shake the thermometer so that the mercury level is well down.
- Lubricate it with a little Vaseline.
- Stand to one side of the horse (the left side if you are right-handed) and raise its tail out of the way with one hand.
- Insert the thermometer into and close to the side of the rectum, keeping a firm grip on the end as horses sometimes exert suction and can draw the thermometer right inside.
- Hold for one minute then withdraw and read the result.

The normal temperature range is 37.4–38.4°C (99.5–101.5°F). The horse should quickly become used to having its pulse and temperature taken.

Massage encourages the horse to relax when being handled as well as having therapeutic effects. There are several books available on massage techniques and ten minutes per day is ten minutes well spent. Methods such as the Tellington touch, devised by Linda Tellington-Jones, also make the horse more aware of its own body. If a horse does not like having its mouth and eyes examined, these techniques used to massage the nostrils, lips and gums and around the eyes can overcome the problem.

An examination for lameness requires the horse to trot out in hand. All horses should learn to do this willingly as part of their basic education. Set the horse up, straight and looking in the direction you want to go. Hold the leadrope about 30 cm (1 ft) from the horse's head, with the slack in your other hand. Look straight ahead, not at the horse and give the command 'Trot', firmly and encouragingly. If the horse is reluctant or does not understand, you can have someone else encourage it from behind, taking care to stay out of the way of being kicked. As you run out, keep a steady pace in time with the horse's stride and continue to look straight ahead. Do not be tempted to look at the horse, as this has the effect of making it slow, jib, or even stop. Once the horse is moving well, release the leadrope from the hand nearest the head. It is important for the vet to be able to watch the horse trotting with its head free to move with its stride. At the end of the trot, slow progressively, stop, turn the horse away from

you, that is, so that the horse remains between you and the vet, then trot back in the same way.

Handling the horse for treatment

You cannot always depend on a person visiting your horse having a good understanding of horse psychology! Ideally, a stranger meeting your horse for the first time, especially if they are used to working with horses, should approach the horse quietly and give it a chance to smell and look at them carefully before attempting to do whatever they are there to do. Unfortunately, some people are impatient, or too busy to wait and, if this is the case, it is even more important for you to be able to reassure your horse that everything is all right and no one is going to hurt it (even if, as in some veterinary procedures, this is not strictly true).

The general rule of safety is that the handler should stand on the same side of the horse as the person treating it, unless instructed otherwise. If the horse jumps away, you are then in no danger of being squashed against the stable wall.

The horse should be comfortably restrained, only to such a degree as is necessary. If you begin by grabbing hold of the headcollar and yelling 'Stand!', the horse will immediately become alert and aware that something it may not like is going to happen. As previously mentioned, horses are uncomfortable when their head movement is restricted, so keep this excuse for tension to the minimum. For example, if the vet needs to give an intravenous injection, simply hold the leadrope under the chin, but do not pull on it or take up any tension unless the horse does so first, as the horse will always react against any pull on its head, which just makes the job more difficult. If the horse does try to pull away, go with it rather than pulling back, then quietly move the head back where you want it. Stay in close to give the horse confidence and talk quietly to it. The more calm and at ease you are, the more readily the horse will accept whatever is done.

Stay alert to what the person treating the horse is doing, so that if you need to move quickly, or help, you can do so. If you are uncertain of what you should do, do not be afraid to ask. Vets, in particular, may often have to put themselves in a position of risk and may be handling equipment that is fragile or potentially dangerous, so allow them to concentrate and do not distract them with inconsequential matters.

Routine treatments

Vaccinations

Giving vaccinations against equine influenza and tetanus is the simplest of the visiting veterinary surgeon's routine tasks, taking only a few seconds. Just hold the horse as described above, staying calm and relaxed and the intramuscular injection will be given in the chest or the rump before the horse even realises what is happening.

A few horses react violently against the prospect of an injection, or against the presence of the vet, usually due to mis-handling in the past. If you know that your horse is likely to react in this way, warn the vet. He can then take the extra time needed to let the horse get used to his presence and to reassure it, before attempting any actual treatment. The vet may gently thump the muscle a few times before quickly inserting the needle. This has the effect of desensitising the area and decreasing the horse's anticipation of unpleasantness or pain. By the time the horse becomes aware of the actual prick, the injection has been given. The use of a twitch should not be necessary for routine vaccinations, except in extreme circumstances.

At times, the vet may need to take a blood sample or give an intravenous injection, requiring the needle to be inserted into the jugular vein. The handler should turn the horse's head slightly so that the neck is bent away from the vet and he can raise the vein more easily. Again, most horses accept the process calmly.

Teeth

The horse's teeth need regular inspections, at least once a year or more frequently for young and elderly horses. This is to ensure that the rate and pattern of wear is not causing difficulty with the bit nor in masticating food. The horse's teeth continue to grow throughout its life and are worn down by grinding food. However, the upper jaw is normally slightly wider than the lower jaw, so that hooks or ridges form on the outer edge of the upper teeth and inner edge of the lower teeth. These can cause ulcers or lacerations in the cheeks or tongue, with resultant pain, difficulty in chewing and resistance to the bit. The vet can check for other dental problems, such as wolf teeth, loose teeth, or infections at the same time.

The only effective way for the vet to see and feel inside the horse's mouth is to hold it open using a 'gag'. This is a metal device which fits over the teeth, is held on by a leather strap over the poll and opens the mouth with a ratchet system. Most horses accept it quite readily. Once the mouth is held open and the vet has inspected the teeth, he can perform any necessary work with the gag in place.

The headcollar must be loosened around the jaw for the mouth to open fully. The handler should stand to one side, with the horse loosely restrained so that the vet has the freedom to move around the horse's head. The handler must stay alert for any sudden movements by the horse, as the gag is a heavy, solid piece of equipment which can cause a nasty injury should it hit the handler's face.

Horses unaccustomed to the procedure of tooth rasping may back away, shake or twist their heads away, or half rear at first. A little patience and perseverance on the part of both vet and handler usually results in the horse settling down and accepting the procedure. Tooth rasping itself is not painful and some horses even appear to enjoy it, possibly due to an endorphin effect. However, if the dental treatment is likely to be painful or protracted, or the horse is particularly nervous the vet may decide to give a light sedative. In this case the handler may need to support the horse's head, so that the vet can continue the treatment.

Giving medicines

By mouth

Medicines are given either orally, by syringe or in the feed, or by injection. All horse owners need to know how to give an anthelmintic (de-worming) preparation by syringe as this is something you will do regularly throughout your horse's life.

Have the headcollar adjusted to a reasonably secure fit – it is much easier to control a horse in a headcollar if the noseband is adjusted to fit rather than being left too loose, as is often the case when the same headcollar is used for a number of horses of varying sizes. Adjust the ring on the plunger of the syringe to give the correct dosage, then remove the cap from the nozzle. Stand to one side of the horse and either slip your free hand under its chin and over its nose or, if the horse dislikes this, gently take hold of the headcollar at the side of the nose on the side nearest to you. Some horses will open their mouths at pressure from the nozzle of the syringe. However, some are wary of the syringe, anticipating something unpleasant and pull away instead. If your horse is one of these, rub the corner of the lips with your thumb, then gently insert it into the mouth to encourage the horse to open it, as if you were inserting a bit. You can then slip the syringe in. Slide it fully into the mouth, and deposit the paste as far back on the tongue as possible. The key to doing this successfully is to be well organised and quick. Few horses enjoy the taste of wormers and it is always more difficult if you have to have a second attempt.

If giving wormers is a problem, you can practise and, at the same time encourage your horse to accept the process more readily, by filling a spent syringe with apple sauce and administering it daily for a few days. The horse will come to associate the syringe with the pleasant taste of the apple sauce. He may not enjoy being fooled with the real worming preparation a few days later, but you can always return to giving apple sauce for a few more days until he forgives you!

Some medicines, such as anti-inflammatory and painkilling drugs are formulated to be given in the feed. There is obviously no problem in administration, provided the horse eats the food. Unfortunately, the taste often puts a fussy horse off. These drugs can usually be given in alternative forms, or can be mixed with a suitable carrier (apple sauce or syrup) and given by syringe, so if you have a problem with a horse refusing to take medicine in its food, ask your vet for an alternative suggestion. You can then be sure that your horse gets the appropriate dose and that you are not just wasting your money.

Injections

Intra-muscular injections are the only type that a horse owner may be expected to administer. The usual scenario is when the horse needs a three-or

five-day course of antibiotics and they are usually given in the large muscles of the rump, using alternate sides on alternate days. Have the horse tied up safely, or held by a helper standing on the same side as the person giving the injection. Stand close at the side of the horse, facing towards the rear, so that you are out of harm's way should the horse kick out. Hold the needle, detached from the syringe, between thumb and forefinger. With the heel of your hand give three or four rapid thumps on the area where the needle will be inserted, then quickly, in the same rhythm, turn your hand and push the needle in. If this is done efficiently, the horse will not even be aware of the needle. Check that there is no blood flowing back through the needle. This occasionally happens if you hit a blood vessel, in which case the needle must be removed and reinserted. Attach the syringe and, holding the top of the needle firmly with one hand, depress the plunger with the other until the syringe is empty. For a thick antibiotic solution, this will take a few seconds, so be ready to go with the horse's movement if it does step away.

First aid and injuries

Unfortunately, accidental injury to the horse is a common occurrence and, sooner or later, anyone involved with horses is going to have to deal with such a situation. The first essential is to remain calm, so that you can both reassure the horse and make an objective appraisal of the damage. If the horse can safely be moved to a stable or other quiet environment, away from traffic and crowds, do so. Otherwise, create a clear space around the animal, take any necessary steps to ensure the safety of others (for example, put out warning signs or people to direct traffic away from an accident on the road) and send any unnecessary bystanders away. If the injuries appear serious, or the horse is in shock, or there is a risk of internal damage, send for the vet immediately. The signs of shock include a dazed apparance, weak or rapid pulse rate and pale mucous membranes. The consequences can be fatal if urgent treatment is not given.

Bleeding usually stops quite quickly unless from an artery, in which case immediate veterinary attention is needed. A correctly applied pressure bandage can help arrest bleeding until the vet arrives. The prevention of infection is critical in obtaining fast, clean healing and the more quickly treatment is given, the less problematic healing will be. A wound treated within minutes of injury will have a far better chance of healing by first intention (i.e., by straightforward knitting together), than the same wound unattended for several hours. Dirty wounds, such as broken knees, benefit from continuous cold hosing, for up to 30 minutes, while awaiting veterinary help.

An injured horse derives considerable comfort from the presence of someone it knows and trusts and the handler can also make sure that the horse moves as little as possible until the vet arrives to assess the full extent of any injuries. An injured horse waiting for the vet will quickly become cold, even on quite a warm day, so use rugs or blankets to keep it warm and help guard against shock.

Nursing

The importance of hygiene in managing the stabled horse recovering from illness or injury cannot be stressed too strongly. Dust is an ever present enemy to the horse's health and clean, dust-free bedding with regular skipping out and removal of wet material is essential, while feed and water bowls, clothing, and grooming kit should all be kept as clean as possible.

Daily records of vital signs such as pulse and temperature, normality of droppings etc. should be kept so that changes in the horse's condition can be monitored. Dressings should be changed as directed by the veterinary surgeon.

Most horses accept the treatment of wounds of quite painful appearance with little objection. In fact the granulation tissue which develops as part of the healing process contains few nerve endings and washing and re-dressing is seldom difficult. Effective bandaging requires practice as it needs to be tight enough to remain in place, smooth enough to avoid uneven pressure and not so tight that it interferes with the circulation or causes pressure damage. If you have to refit bandages, ask your vet to show you how to obtain the correct tension and

also how to fit bandages over joints, etc so that they stay in place. Ideally, use proprietory hock, knee or fetlock bandages which zip up over the wound dressings and inner bandage and do not move.

If a horse becomes fractious or difficult about having dressings removed or replaced, the handler must be patient and persevere in gaining the horse's co-operation quietly and calmly, whilst insisting that bad behaviour will not be tolerated (see Chapter 12 for dealing with problems). Often, the removal of dressings which have become dried on or stuck to the wound, or of Elastoplast, can be more difficult than fitting new dressings. Avoid tying up a horse which is likely to struggle or panic in this situation. Make sure the stable is safe and remove any loose or unnecessary buckets, utensils, etc. Handle the horse exactly as you would for any other stable procedure. Reward good behaviour with rubbing and verbal rewards and avoid struggling with the horse, for example by pulling on the leadrope, or grappling to hold on to a leg when the horse has pulled away. Be patient and persistent and lavishly reward each small piece of progress towards your goal.

Rehabilitation

Controlled exercise is often prescribed for horses recovering from injuries such as tendon strain and this is sometimes easier said than done. The horse that has been confined to a stable for some time becomes excited as soon as it is led outside. The desire for grass, which has been denied while the horse has been stabled, often overcomes the inclination to leap about, so if you can lead the horse out to graze initially this may help. Use of a controller halter, so that you can more easily restrain the horse's exuberance is also a good idea. If the horse has been trained to long rein and can be restrained to a walk, this is an ideal way of obtaining controlled exercise without weight on its back, when lungeing on a circle would be inadvisable due to putting too much strain on the recovering limb. Alternatively, try corralling the horse within electric fencing in a small area not much bigger than a stable at first and progressively increasing the size.

Chapter 4

Tack and Equipment

Fitting of tack

We should remember that the horse is a sensitive creature as much when we are on the ground as when riding. It is unfair to reprimand a horse for 'bad' behaviour when it is justifiably reacting to the discomfort of badly fitted tack, or to the prospect of being inconsiderately bridled or saddled. Many people are simply unaware of the effect their tack has on the horse's body, particularly the saddle. The horse may suffer for a long time before the problem becomes too serious to ignore, whether it is a simple girth gall, or long-term muscle damage. The effects can be far reaching. Horses often alter their gait to compensate for saddle discomfort, thus putting strain on joints and ligaments. If the shortened or uneven action goes unnoticed because there is no obvious lameness, the damage becomes chronic and maybe irreversible, with the horse mutely suffering perhaps for years until arthritis leads to retirement on the grounds of old age!

Bridles, for the most part, are easily adjusted and only a few rules need be followed. However, the browband is not adjustable and these are frequently too short and thus too tight for comfort. The browband should lie about 2.5 cm (1 in) below the base of the ears, and should be long enough to fit around the forehead without pulling the headband forwards and without impinging on the sensitive base of the ears. A tight browband is extremely uncomfortable and no horse can be blamed for rubbing and head shaking in an effort to get rid of it.

The throatlatch keeps the bridle from falling off when the horse's head is lowered and it must be fitted with three to four fingers breadth between it and the throat, leaving it loose enough to avoid restricting the horse's breathing when it flexes at the poll.

The cheek pieces are adjusted so that a snaffle bit just wrinkles the corners of the mouth, leaving the mouthpiece neither uncomfortably high, nor so low that it bangs against the teeth. A horse can easily get its tongue over a bit that is fitted too low. If this happens when the horse is ridden it will raise and toss its head and be completely unresponsive to the rein aids. The bit must be re-fitted correctly before the horse is ridden on, but if the problem persists, the horse must be re-trained (see Chapter 12).

Straight-bar bits are usually fitted slightly lower than jointed bits. The width of the bit is also important. The mouthpiece should emerge for approximately 6 mm (0.25 in) either side of the lips before joining the cheeks. If it is too narrow, it will pinch the lips; if too wide, it will slide through the mouth and rub, or even bruise, the lips and gums. Unfortunately, many popular bits today are made in a narrow range of sizes, and you may have to search to find exactly the right fit.

Cavesson nosebands should be fitted with two fingers' space between the noseband and jaw, below and well clear of the protuberances of the cheekbones, but high enough to avoid interfering with the action of the bit. A useful ploy to stop a young horse opening its mouth, without resorting to the more severe drop noseband, is to fit the cavesson slightly lower and tighter than normal.

The flash noseband is basically a cavesson with an extra strap passing under the jaw below the bit. Its effect is to keep the horse's mouth closed and bring a little more downward pressure to bear to encourage a young horse to lower its head, enabling it to adopt a more correct outline. Make sure you can insert two fingers between the lower strap and the jaw, when it is fastened. Most horses accept the flash without objection but a particularly sensitive youngster may dislike it.

The drop noseband is commonly seen on heavier types of horse and ponies that pull. Its effect of momentarily interfering with the breathing encourages the horse to lower its head and thereby allow a rider to regain control. Correctly fitted, it

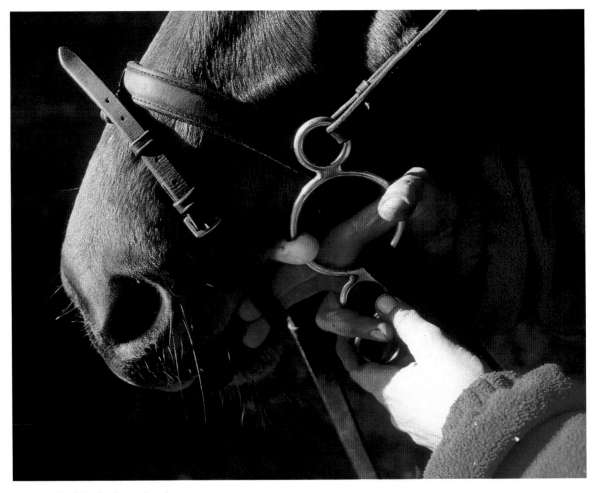

Correct fit of the flash noseband.

lies on the lower, softer part of the nasal bones, about 7.5 cm (3 in) above the nostrils, with the back strap below the bit lying in the curb groove. Before you use this noseband to counteract pulling, remember that the horse can only pull if the rider pulls back – ask yourself if there is not a better or more effective way to solve the problem.

There are various other nosebands and bridles. When fitting them, the basic rule is to ensure the comfort of the horse. Avoid any straps coming too close to the eyes, buckles fastened in positions where they will rub, bit shanks that dig into the side of the horse's face, or nosebands so low that they lie on the soft part of the nose, permanently restricting breathing.

The correct fit of the saddle is a subject that has received a great deal of attention in recent years,

perhaps due to the growth of interest in riding as a leisure activity and also to the increasingly precise demands of riders in competitive sports, such as dressage and endurance. Correct saddle fitting today combines the revival of an almost lost art with the benefits of scientific research and modern technology. When horses were a vital part of every day life, in civilian transport as well as military operations, a saddle that did not cause sores and result in the horse having to be rested was essential.

Once horses were replaced by motor vehicles and used only for sport and pleasure, the comfort of the rider for hunting and jumping tended to take precedence over that of the horse. The horse was usually only ridden for fairly short periods at a time, so it might take months for any damage to become physically obvious, by which time it would be chronic, rather than acute, in nature. How many horses do you see with patches of white hair at the withers which have developed as a result of perhaps years of short periods of pressure?

The growth of endurance riding was one catalyst that encouraged research into this problem, as more and more riders found that a saddle which apparently fitted well would begin to cause pressure sores once the horse was competing over 40 miles or more in a day. It was realised that in fact the horse was feeling discomfort and that its performance could be severely compromised, long before physical evidence of poor saddle fit was seen. Riders in other disciplines, particularly dressage, where the horse's comfort is essential if it is to perform gymnastic movements well, took up the problem and various manufacturers, some new on the scene, some traditional saddle-makers, began to produce saddles which met the necessary criteria of comfort and humane fit.

Scientific research, using techniques such as thermography and computer-aided measurement of pressure, helped in producing the optimum designs.

The principal requirements of a well-fitting saddle are:

a) **The tree should be of the correct width, that is, neither so wide that it presses down on the spine, nor so narrow that the points pinch on either side of the withers. It must also be of a suitable length – long enough to accommodate the rider and short enough to avoid concentrating weight on the loins.**

b) **The weight-bearing area, whether conventional stuffed panels or one of the new adjustable or conformable designs, must be as extensive as possible in order to spread the rider's weight over a large area of the back muscles and minimise the pressure at any one point.**

c) **The panels of the saddle must conform longitudinally to the shape of the horse's back. A common fault, diagnosed with the aid of computer technology, is bridging, where the saddle sits on the back fore and aft, but leaves a gap in the middle, so that weight is** concentrated at the points where contact is made and causes friction and soreness. The broader and flatter the panel surface, the greater the weight-bearing area. Various methods are used to overcome this problem including re-flocking of conventional panels (which may not be broad enough anyway), the use of materials which mould to the shape of the back, the provision of removable extra pads of various shapes to build up the correct fit (an expert job which is often left to the inexperienced owner!), and the invention of 'floating' or 'suspended' panels, which aim to allow the horse greater freedom of movement by virtue of the fact that the panels are able to move independently of one another, as the horse moves each side of its back.

d) **The latter point in (c) also has an effect on the need for the saddle to avoid any inhibition of the horse's ability to move freely and naturally. This is a tall order, given that we are imposing an unnatural situation on the horse in the first place. However, it is essential, for the sake of the horse's comfort and, as we have already said, an uncomfortable horse cannot be blamed for 'bad' behaviour. Basically, the requirement here is that the saddle should fit so that the horse can move freely without having to alter or inhibit its way of going to avoid pain or discomfort due to having a rider on board. Common problem areas include pressure points behind the withers under the stirrup bars, a tree that is too wide and allows the saddle to press on the structures above the spine, or pressure caused by bridging. Friction under the cantle can be caused by side to side movement of a saddle which does not properly conform to the horse's back, or by the seat being unlevel and tipping down so that the rider sits on the back of the seat. Finally, the shoulder action can be inhibited due to the points hitting the back of the scapula as the horse stretches the leg forwards.**

It is important to realise that the repetitive movements of the horse in action will not necessarily show up any problems immediately. Their development is insidious in nature and by the time they become physically evident, if indeed they ever do to the inexperienced eye, much damage has been done. The horse, if being used for competitive sports, will have been performing well below the level of its full potential, with inevitable disappointments for the rider, probably ever since the saddle was first used.

These points cover the fit of the saddle for the horse. It is also important that the saddle is correctly designed to allow the rider to ride in balance. Surprisingly, many saddles, especially general purpose saddles, do not do this. However, many back problems in horses begin because the rider is not properly balanced. We will consider this further in Chapter 6.

Test the fit of your saddle

It is possible to ride on a correctly fitting saddle without the use of a numnah. However, a well-designed numnah provides extra cushioning if the horse is being ridden for long periods and also protects the leather panels from sweat and dirt. A good numnah is one which can be pulled up into the gullet to avoid pressure on the spine and is still big enough to sit clear of the back of the panels. It must not wrinkle, which would cause uneven pressure and it must not 'draw' the back or cause excessive build up of heat under the saddle, as some synthetic fabrics do. There are some excellent modern synthetics, but wool and cotton are still unbeatable choices.

Girths come in many designs and materials. Our favourite is the Saint girth, designed for endurance riding, which is made of strong webbing with separate liners of neoprene or cotton padding covered with absorbent fleece. The liners are attached to the girth with broad touch-and-close fastening. Thus the same girth can be used throughout a long ride by changing the liner at each stop. The liners can be machine washed, while the girth itself needs only a quick scrub.

Synthetic materials such as neoprene make good girth coverings, while traditional leather and lampwick are also good. The most important thing about any girth is that it should be clean, soft and supple to avoid causing rubs and galls.

(Narrow panels) Weight-bearing area too small.

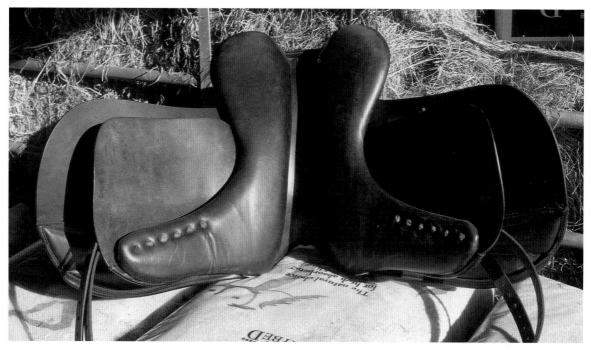

(Good saddle) Broad weight-bearing panels.

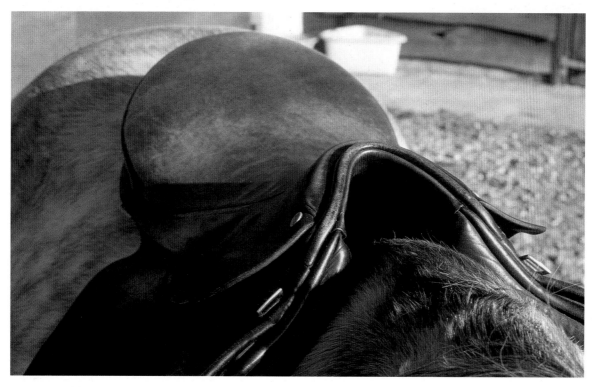

(Narrow saddle on broad horse) Tree too narrow.

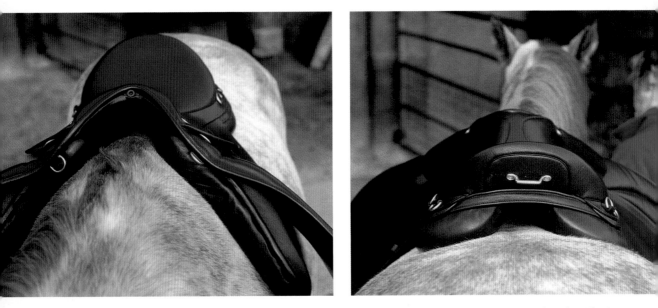

(Good saddle) A correctly fitting tree. This must be checked when the saddle is girthed up and again when the rider is on board as the saddle will settle considerably with the weight of the rider. Clearance of spine both along length and width.

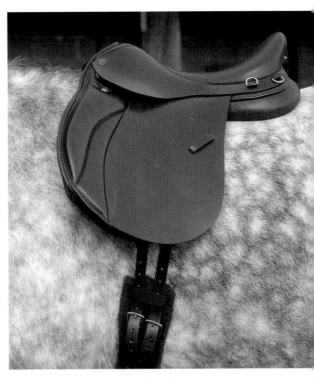

(Poor fit) This saddle is too narrow and moves laterally at the back, which would cause friction under the back of the saddle.

Correct flocking or panel design ensures the saddle seat is level. Too high at the front or back gives the rider a feeling of going 'uphill' or 'downhill' and makes it impossible to ride in balance

Tacking up

The saddle

A calm horse can be tacked up untied in the stable, but if you are at all uncertain of the horse or of your own ability to do the job efficiently, the horse is best tied up. If the horse is tied, we put the saddle on first; if not, you can start with either saddle or bridle. If the horse is inclined to walk away from the saddle, it can be trained to stand (see Chapter 11), but meanwhile, tie it up instead until it has learnt to accept the process more willingly.

A numnah can either be fitted to the saddle first, or placed on the horse's back and then attached to the saddle as appropriate. In the latter case, let the horse see the numnah before you throw it over its back. In either case, make sure the numnah is well pulled up into the gullet of the saddle before girthing up.

Before saddling up, check that the stirrups are run up securely and the girth, if attached, is folded over the saddle, or, if a dressage girth is used, through the stirrup. Assuming the horse is tied up, approach it with the saddle over your left arm, then stop and allow the horse to look at and sniff the saddle to reassure itself that this is a familiar object of which

it need have no fear. Many saddling problems develop purely because the horse has never been allowed an opportunity to familiarise itself with this heavy, if inanimate, monster which it suddenly finds dumped on its back and which it then cannot even see. How does the horse know the saddle is not dangerous? We will look further at introducing the saddle to a young horse in Chapter 11.

When you have shown the saddle to the horse and assuming it shows no fear, move along the horse's side and lift the saddle on to its back, placing it well forward initially, without bumping, and then sliding it back into position so that the hairs lie flat underneath. Check the position of the numnah and go quietly to the off side and let down the girth. Return to the near side and, placing your left hand on the horse's shoulder for reassurance, reach under the belly and bring the girth up for fastening. Be careful not to startle the horse, particularly if it is sensitive or nervous, when you reach under its belly. Slide the back of your hand down and under, along the girth area, before picking up the girth, and then slide your hand back up with it so that the horse knows what is happening. Fasten it quite loosely at first, just touching the horse. The girth should be tightened

a

ABOVE and OVERLEAF: Saddling sequence: *a) Placing the saddle blanket.*

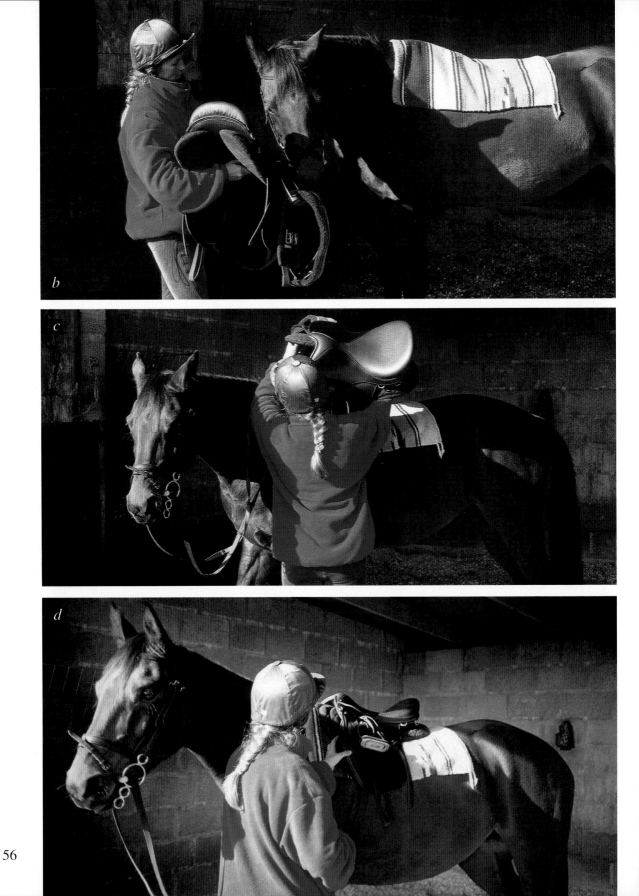

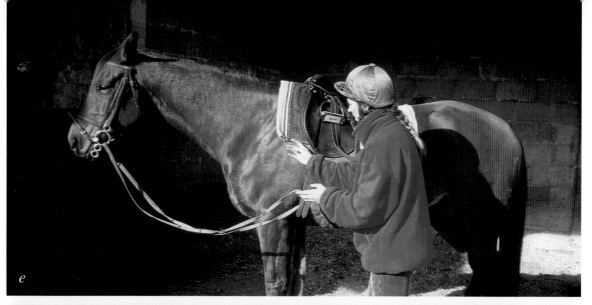

e

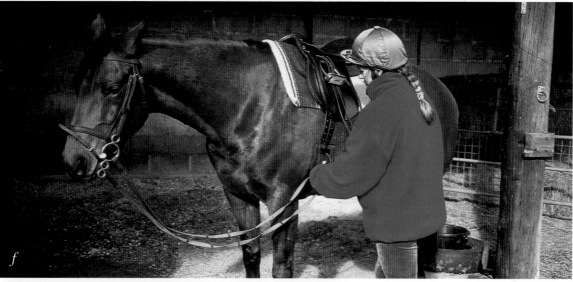

f

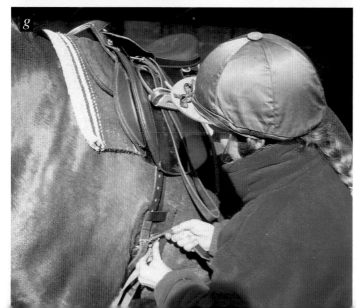

g

OPPOSITE & THIS PAGE:
Saddling sequence:

b) Showing the horse the saddle.

c) Lifting the saddle on to the horse's back. Tammy experienced some saddle problems in the past and is inclined to move away from the saddle – note the foreleg beginning to move.

d) & e) The saddle on the horse. Becky is working on asking her to stand still.

f) & g) Fastening the girth. Do this on both sides and one hole at a time.

gently in stages, one hole at a time, in between moving around the horse to put on the rest of its tack. As you tighten the girth, pull the straps outwards away from the horse, rather than directly upwards, to avoid any risk of pinching the skin between the strap and the buckle. Do not try to tighten the girth to the last possible hole on the ground. This is better done from the saddle when your weight will have settled the saddle anyway and it will be easier to make the final fastening.

To ensure that there is no skin pinched or wrinkled under the girth, you can lift the horse's forelegs one at a time, or simply ask it to walk forward a few steps before you mount.

h) & i) We overcame Tammy's saddle fitting problems with this flat-panelled 'Free 'n' Easy' saddle which has a very broad weight-bearing surface and flexible, independent panels.

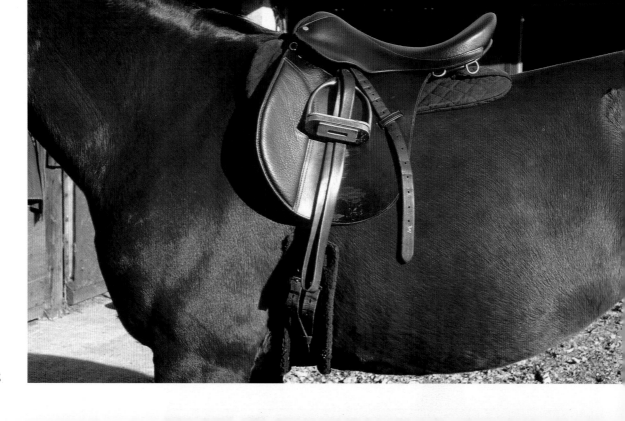

The bridle

Horses react to being bridled in various ways. After all, how would you like a chunk of cold steel forcibly inserted in your mouth! A well-trained horse will accept the bridle calmly, if not always opening its mouth willingly. If there is a problem with bridling a horse, it is because the job has been inconsiderately done in the past and the horse must be re-trained to accept the bit without a struggle, in the same way as for a young horse (see Chapter 11).

Of course the bit need not, these days, be a chunk of cold steel. Kinder metals, such as sweet

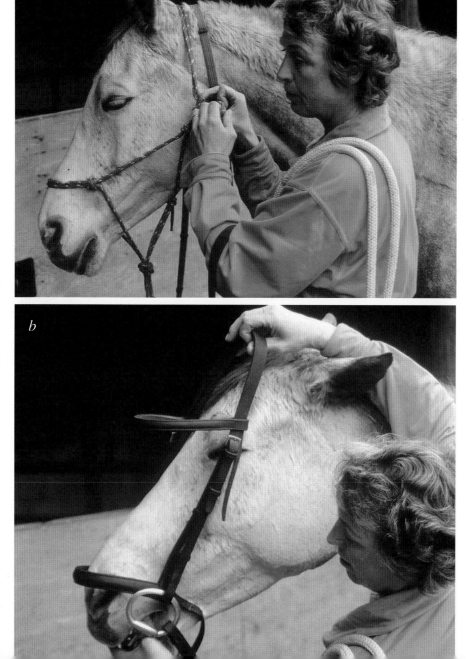

Bridling Sequence:
a) The reins are placed over the neck. Unfasten the headcollar and re-fasten it around the horse's neck, or remove it altogether.

b) The reins are placed over the neck. The bridle is taken in the right hand over the horse's nose, with the bit in the palm of the left hand. Rubbing the side of the lips, inserting the thumb between the bars and if necessary tickling the roof of the mouth will encourage a reluctant horse to open its mouth.

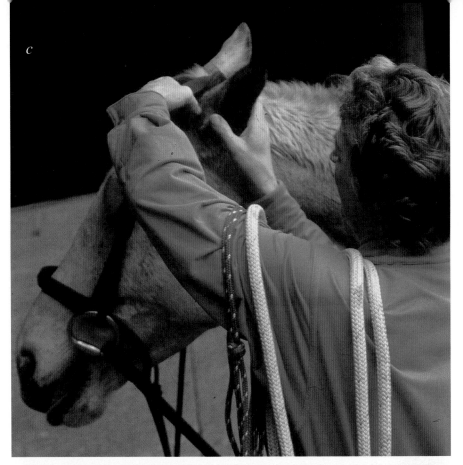

c) The headpiece is lifted carefully over the ears.

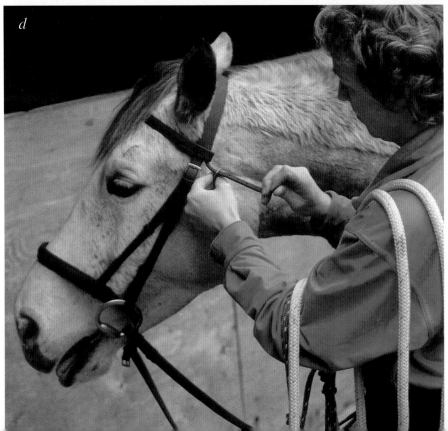

d) The throatlatch, noseband and, if any, curb chain are correctly fastened in succession.

60

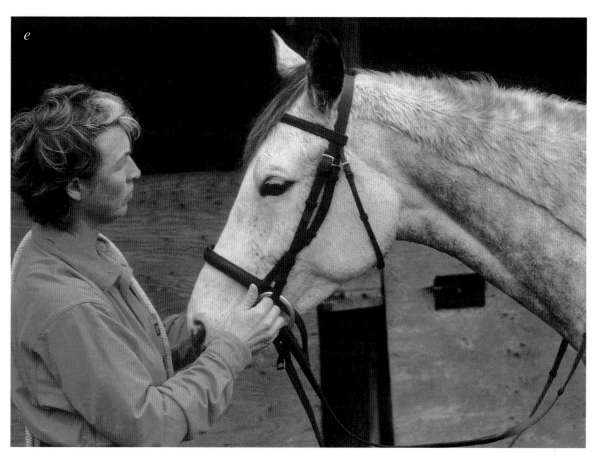

e

e) Checking for comfort and fit.

iron, or copper and its alloys are said to feel warmer and also to encourage salivation – a wet mouth is a more sensitive and giving mouth when the horse is ridden. Alternatively, many horses are much happier in the synthetic bits made of polyurethane, which exert a more gentle pressure on the mouth. Finally, there is always old-fashioned rubber, which we find useful for youngsters being bitted for the first time provided their mouths are not too small to take the thickness of a rubber bit.

Vulcanite found favour for several years, usually in a mullen-mouth design, but it does tend to be hard and ungiving and again, rather thick for many horses' mouths.

The following procedure is used to bridle a horse:

• **Approach the horse in the normal way, with the headpiece of the bridle over the fingers of your left hand and the reins over your arm.**
• **Slip the reins over the horse's head.**
• **Unfasten the headcollar and re-fasten it around the horse's neck, or remove it altogether.**
• **Stand beside the horse's head, take the headpiece in your right hand and the bit in your left hand, with the noseband clear of the bit on either side.**
• **Offer the bit to the horse's mouth on the flat of your palm, at the same time bringing the headpiece up over the horse's nose. A horse that is easy to bridle will accept the bit and you can then raise the headpiece in your right hand, while your left hand guides the ears through in turn.**
• **Check the bridle for fit and ensure that the browband is correctly positioned.**
• **Fasten the throatlatch, then the noseband,**

61

bringing the straps of the noseband inside the cheekpieces.

Many horses are less obliging and refuse to open their mouths for the bit when it is offered in this way. If this is the case, adopt a slightly different procedure. As before, take the bit in your left hand, but hold the bridlework shorter with your right hand around the cheeks and holding the noseband up. Instead of moving your right hand up the front of the horse's face, take it under the jaw and over the nose from the far side. This enables you to stay closer to the horse, discourages it from moving away from your upraised arm and allows you to place your right hand with the bridle supported, on the horse's nose to help your left hand guide the bit into place. Offer the bit across the fingers of your left hand and, as you do so, slide your thumb into the mouth in the gap where the bit lies between the molars and incisors. The horse will usually open its mouth in response, but if not, gentle rubbing of the roof of the mouth with your thumb will usually do the trick. You can then slip the bit in, while holding up the bridle, then switch hands and guide the headpiece over the ears as before.

A tip when bridling and unbridling: check that none of the straps are twisted before fastening and always do things in the same order. When bridling, fasten the throatlatch first, then the noseband, then the curb chain, if any and when unbridling, do it all in reverse order. This way, nothing is omitted and the horse becomes familiar with the routine.

Equipment for schooling from the ground

Depending upon the aim and the level of work you want to do, this can be anything from a simple rope halter to the full works of lungeing cavesson, bridle, roller and breastplate, side-reins and boots. The usual reason for the leisure horse owner to want to school from the ground is to lunge the horse when, for some reason, it cannot be ridden, so we will take a look at fitting lungeing equipment.

The most readily available and economical lungeing cavesson is the nylon type, with two straps under the jaw and a padded noseband. This has three rings on the noseband, but only the central

one is used for lungeing. The lungeing cavesson must be fitted snugly to the head, with the noseband approximately one finger's width below the cheekbone and the straps fastened securely enough to prevent the cavesson from being pulled across the horse's outside eye when lungeing. The noseband is fitted underneath the bridle to allow the bit to move freely. The headpiece goes over the bridle and lies over the top or just behind the bridle headpiece. The middle jawstrap can lie either over or under the bridle cheekpieces, whichever is most comfortable. The lunge line attaches to the front, central ring of the cavesson and the swivel must turn freely.

A roller is a padded surcingle with rings fitted for rein attachment; it is used with a normal girth. For comfort and to avoid any risk of pinching the withers, it should always be used with a wither pad or saddle blanket. A lampwick, or elasticated girth, which has a little give in it and is more comfortable when the horse moves, is ideal. We frequently see horses being lunged in rollers without breastplates – this is a dangerous practice as if the roller slips back to the horse's loins you will have a frantic, bucking, kicking, terrified horse on your hands. Any type of breastplate can be used, but do not lunge without one.

Once a horse is accustomed to lungeing, side-reins help to keep it straight and in a more correct outline. They should be fitted the same length each side and can be fastened to either the side rings on the cavesson or directly to the bit. In a trained horse, the latter is usual and should be easily accepted. We like to allow the horse to warm up without the side-reins. They must be attached very loosely at first, until the horse is accustomed to them, as you will achieve nothing if you try to force the horse's head into place – this will only cause tension in the neck muscles. The reins can be shortened gradually over a number of lungeing sessions, as the horse accepts the contact. At the end of the session, unclip the side reins immediately to let the horse relax and stretch its neck.

The horse's legs should always be protected with boots for lungeing, as the action of a horse on the lunge is often less inhibited than when encumbered by a rider. Apart from the possibility of brushing, or a hind foot striking into a foreleg, there is also the chance of injury if a horse shies or panics while on the lunge. Boots are preferable to bandages as they offer more substantial protection and there is no risk of them tripping the horse up if they become undone. There are many inexpensive boots available today, often lined with neoprene, which is soft and does not rub. Boots should be washed after each use to prevent the development of rubs and sweat rashes.

The most important aspect of a lunge whip is that it should be well balanced and easy to use without your wrist becoming tired. It should be about 2.4 m (8 ft) long with a 1.8 m (6 ft) lash. This gives enough length to be able to control the horse without making your lungeing circle too small.

Finally, as always, the handler should wear gloves and a hard hat, for protection and safety, plus suitable footwear.

Lungeing itself is an art and it is worth asking an experienced person to show you the various methods and how to school your horse effectively in this way. There is far more to it than just getting the horse to go round in circles. The way you handle the lunge line and whip and where you position yourself will make the difference between achieving something worthwhile, in terms of improving your horse's way of going, helping to build up its muscles, top-line and self-carriage, and just making the horse tired! Poor lungeing technique also puts a great strain on the horse's joints and, if done to excess, will result in incorrect muscle development.

Long reining is a very useful way of schooling a horse without a rider on board and is very under used. The equipment used is much the same as for lungeing, with an extra rein and, as with lungeing, there are several different techniques. It can be done on a circle, but also has the benefit of versatility – you can perform numerous figures with changes of direction in the arena, or go out for a 'hack'.

Asking horses to work in hand

There are many forms of in-hand work, apart from lungeing and long reining, limited only by the imagination of the handler. Horse owners seldom

Desert Rose kitted out for long reining. (For more photos of ground work, see Chapter 11).

seem interested in pursuing these exercises or 'games' as some trainers prefer to call them, which is a great pity as they will teach you, as well as your horse, a great deal and give you a much better understanding of the horse's character.

At the very least, a horse should be responsive to the basic requests to move forwards, backwards and sideways in hand without fuss or resistance. Other 'games' include familiarisation with strange obstacles – poles, tyres, flapping plastic or washing, umbrellas, bicycles, etc. So often you hear people comment that their horse will not go near pigs, umbrellas or some other imagined danger, but all such fears can be overcome with the appropriate form of conditioning.

The most basic lessons for in-hand work are simply a continuation of those the horse learned in the stable – they require the horse to be aware of the handler's presence and position and respond to him or her in an acceptable way. Horses that barge around in the stable are often those that misbehave outside, for example, when being saddled up at a show. In conjunction with this, you hear the frustrated owner yelling sharply and completely ineffectively at the poor animal to 'Stand still!' Frustration often leads to loss of temper, or at least to loss of self-control. The yelling is then accompanied by actions such as grabbing the horse's bridle and yanking at the mouth, pulling it around, thumping the quarters and making the sort of quick, thoughtless movements that startle, upset and confuse a horse, so that the problem just becomes worse.

The place to teach a horse basic in-hand behaviour is in your yard at home. More interesting games can be played in an arena or paddock with a few items such as poles, tyres, barrels, plastic bags, etc. Avoid having too much clutter, however, and make sure any equipment used is safe for the horse.

Introducing these games adds the variety that is often missing from the domesticated horse's life, while increasing its awareness of its own body and its ability to use itself accurately and with athleticism. Negotiating obstacles, such as a maze of poles for example, by controlled movement forwards, backwards and sideways, requires the horse to increase its concentration and to focus its attention on the handler and the signals it receives.

You may have heard it said that a horse can only concentrate on learning or performing in a controlled environment that is quiet and away from other horses. How many times have you heard a disgruntled dressage rider complain, 'That would have been a good test if the tractor (or the cattle, or something else) hadn't started up on the other side of the fence'? The fact is that if your horse is concentrating on you and what you are asking it to do, it does not pay much attention to what else is going on around it. Overcoming the tendency to be influenced by outside distractions and to accept that other horses may be working or playing nearby, or other things happening, is part of the learning process. If you always train your horse in an environment where it is protected from outside influences, it will not be able to handle them when you do go somewhere full of distractions, such as a show. This is why showjumpers that are brought on and do well jumping indoors all winter, often fail abysmally when they have to move outdoors in the spring. They are mentally unprepared for the open spaces and the sights and sounds of the big world outside.

Our youngsters may have their lessons together or separately and are expected to leave, pass and go away from their companions without fuss. Provided the youngster is taught to accept the human handler as 'leader' from an early age, this never causes any problem. It is with the unhandled 3-year-old, which has never been out of its field or away from its companions, that difficulties arise.

When training your horse in hand there are some simple rules to follow:

- **Stay calm and relaxed. Remember that the horse must look to you to be its leader and that it will take its cue from your attitude. If you are het up, nervous or afraid, the horse will be so too. If you are calm, the horse will be calm and attentive too.**
- **Make your requests clear, simple and very consistent, using signals the horse can easily understand. For example, if you want the horse to back up, ask in the same way each time, for example, with steadily**

increasing pressure of your fingers on its chest. Do not press on its chest one day, push its nose the next and pull the headcollar another day. It will just be confused.

- Reward a correct response *instantly* with praise and rubbing the horse's body as appropriate – the part of the body you were pressing, or, if it has come to you, the front of its head. Here is a point to think on: the horse has a blind spot immediately in front of its face, so in allowing you, and even wanting you, to rub its face between the eyes, it is showing an incredible amount of trust and acceptance.

- Make progress slowly and look for quality in each achievement. One small thing well done is worth more than a dozen things badly done. There is fascination in achieving quality and if you concentrate on that, it will prevent you from becoming bored and looking for too many new things to do too quickly.

- Be aware of your horse's powers of concentration. These vary tremendously. A very young horse may be able to concentrate for only a few minutes, while an older, trained horse may be able to work for a couple of hours before becoming mentally tired. However, an older horse that is not accustomed to this kind of work may react in a similar way to the youngster. On the other hand, it might find the exercises so interesting that you will find it calling to you for attention every time you pass the paddock. Listen to your horse; listen to its body language.

- Stay one step ahead of your horse, so you can anticipate its every move and be ready to a) stop giving the aid when it responds correctly, b) reward, or c) counteract a wrong response. When your horse is being attentive to you, your own force of personality should be enough to discourage an unwanted response. You must be quick to react – less than one second. This relationship is a two-way thing that changes between one breath and the next.

- Finally, allow yourself and your horse time. If your horse spooks unexpectedly at something, do not try to hurry past it. Give the horse a chance to stand and look at the offending object. Walk up to the bogey and let the horse follow, so it can sniff and walk around it and prove to itself that there is nothing to fear. A horse that trusts you will invariably follow you where it will not go alone. Even if it does not totally trust you, it will usually rather approach danger with you than be left on its own. Later, when it has developed confidence in you and understands your requests fully, it will approach strange objects without having to follow you, that is, when you are driving it in long reins or riding it.

There are many methods of approaching in-hand work, from traditional, classical schooling to the Monty Roberts 'join-up' method and others expounded by many expert trainers (see the Further Reading list for suggestions). They do not always agree with each other in detail and it is impossible to say that one trainer's method is more 'right' than that of another. They all offer possible approaches to various situations. This book therefore is not going to give you yet another specific programme to follow. We suggest you read, go to demonstrations, experiment and find what suits you and your horse. However, the points listed above are applicable whether you are lungeing, teaching your horse to cope with hazards, or asking it to load into a trailer.

Chapter 5

Loading and Transport

This is an area that frequently causes problems for the less experienced horse owner. The problems fall into two categories: refusal to load and difficulties when travelling. Before we get to that stage, however, there are other points to consider.

Protective clothing

This has become increasingly sophisticated and today the most convenient and fully protective gear for the horse's legs is the 'all in one' travelling boot, which offers protection from above the knees and hocks all the way down to the coronet.

Bandages with separate knee and hock boots can also be used. Some people go to the lengths of putting on over-reach boots to protect the heels, while others simply use bandages and do not worry about hock, knee or coronet protection at all.

The new owner often buys a colour co-ordinated travelling kit with the full works and the first time this is used tends to be when the owner next wants to travel the horse. If the horse is not used to wearing all this gear, the additional clutter attached to its legs can make it very wary, if not nervous and panicked. Remember that the horse has a deeply

Kitted out for travelling on a warm day, Phrizbe wears long boots and a tail bandage.

instinctive need to keep its legs free of encumbrances, to flee from danger and it has no way of knowing that the boots are not a trap. If it decides to get rid of the offending items, touch-and-close fastenings do not stay fastened to kicking legs for long. The flapping, loosened boots then lead to greater panic.

The first rule is to get your horse used to wearing its travelling kit, whatever you choose to use, in the stable. Put the boots on and let the horse move around in this safe environment and get accustomed to them. Do it several times over as many days. If you use a tail guard that needs to be attached to a surcingle, always also use a breastplate to prevent the surcingle from slipping back.

The parts of the horse's leg most in need of protection are the tendons, so when teaching horses to load we fit brushing boots all round instead of the conventional travelling gear. The horse is usually accustomed to them from schooling lessons and, if not, they are more easily accepted than long boots, since they cover a relatively small area, fasten securely and do not move against the horse's own movement. Once the horse understands and accepts what loading and travelling are all about, it is a very easy step to change to proper travelling boots.

Familiarisation

Loading into a lorry or trailer, let alone travelling, is a very unnatural thing for a horse to do. The surprising thing is not that some horses refuse to load, but that so many do so willingly. A horse, being a creature whose safety depends upon the ability to use wide, open spaces for flight, does not willingly walk into a cave, which is what a horsebox represents.

For the horse to accept that the cave might not be dangerous, it must overcome its natural fear of such places. Two things will help the horse to do this: First, it must learn that the cave is quite safe, through a process of conditioning and, second, for the conditioning to be successful, it must trust the person upon whom its responses depend. A horse that has been well trained and well handled should walk into its transport vehicle calmly and on a loose leadrope, either following its handler or being sent on ahead. Unfortunately, life is not always this easy. Refusal to load is not just a problem of young

horses, it can also occur at any time in a horse's life if it has a bad travelling experience, or even if the type of transport is changed, for example, from a lorry to a trailer, or from a light, airy trailer to an old-fashioned, darker one. Conditioning to 'desensitise' the horse so it is no longer afraid of this terrifying, dark box cannot be done in the five minutes before you want to leave for a show. Be prepared to spend days, or, if necessary, weeks to overcome the problem.

In many cases a short amount of time spent coaxing or threatening until a horse is reluctantly half-forced into a box will see it successfully loaded. The tendency of most owners then is to get the ramp up quickly and set off on the journey. They have got the horse loaded this time, but they have not solved the problem and next time the horse will probably be just as difficult, if not more so.

The time to practise loading is when you are not going anywhere and have all day at your disposal. Set the box up in a safe environment. It can help to have at least one side close against a wall to discourage the horse from escaping that way. However, be sure that there is no gap, or other potentially dangerous obstruction, such as a gate, between the wall and the ramp where a horse's leg could slip down and be caught. We have seen horrific injuries caused in this way. A better way, for example, is to reverse the vehicle up to the central walkway of a barn. The fact that there is nowhere to go, either side, helps concentrate the horse's mind on going into the horsebox. If the horsebox is a lorry, with a fairly steep ramp, reverse it uphill so that the ramp levels out. Always ensure that the ramp is lowered on solid ground and does not bounce or give way when weight is put on it. These are just some ways of dealing with particular situations and much depends upon the nature of the horse involved. With young horses, being boxed for the first time, we like to have the box in the open. For older horses, undergoing re-training, we make adjustments to suit the situation and the problem. The two important aims are to make the situation as safe and as easy for the horse as possible.

Many horses dislike loading because of the darkness of the interior of the box. Often, just opening a front door or ramp will be enough to solve the problem.

Loading the horse

There are many different ways in which people have approached this problem and they have varying success. One approach is to make the horse more afraid of what is behind it than what is in front of it. This method includes cracking a lunge whip, prodding the back end with a yard broom, flapping a blanket, or even hitting the horse when it tries to back away from the box. A few horses, usually the less highly bred types, may just respond by shooting into the horsebox to get away from the wolves at their heels. The handlers may have succeeded in loading the horse but they have not overcome its fear, just made it more afraid. They have certainly not gained its respect and understanding and have probably made the problem worse for next time. Even if the method works repeatedly with the same horse, it is not a horseman's solution as it is based on fear and not on trust and understanding.

When this method is tried and fails, it leads to an all-out battle with the horse, resulting in the horse being more determined than ever not to go into that cave. A large, determined horse is more than a match for any number of flapping, shouting humans.

This is a good time to note that whenever a horse refuses to load in a public place, it attracts 'helpers' like bees to a honey-pot, all with different suggestions and all homing in on the horse so that it feels even more confined and trapped. The maximum number of people needed to load a horse is three: one to lead the horse and the other two to help keep it straight by various means (see below) if necessary and to close the ramp when it is finally decided to shut the horse in the box. Send any others away.

For this first loading lesson, the trailer is set up in a clear space with the partition removed and the front ramp open.

A common situation when attempting to load for the first time!

The leadrope is kept slack unless the horse pulls away. A controller halter is useful here for horses that react more strongly. 69

Patience on the part of the handler and curiosity on that of the horse progress the situation further.

Basic loading procedure

Always wear a hard hat and gloves. People have been killed as a result of horses coming backwards out of their transport when the ramp was being shut.

With your trailer or horsebox set up safely and the horse kitted out with the minimum of essential protective clothing, that is, headcollar or halter and brushing boots, lead the horse in a straight line towards the loading ramp. Walk in the same calm, positive manner that you do when leading the horse anywhere. Do not be tentative, so that the horse anticipates stopping and do not adopt a more forceful manner than usual so that the horse wonders what is up. Keep a normal amount of slack in the leadrope. Look where you are going and not at the horse.

A horse that does not want to load will usually stop either at the foot of the ramp or even several

Elf's expression shows both wariness and curiosity, but no fear. She has been well handled and has no cause to distrust humans.

The bucket was tucked away in the trailer ready to give a reward, but Elf is too busy thinking about this new experience. Coming out again poses another problem.

Elf decides to go for it! Note the handler must take care to stand clear of the ramp in case this happens.

Next time round, the jump is reduced to a trot.

British Endurance Team horses get a break at a service station on a long journey through France.

feet away. The mistake that most people then immediately make is to pull on the leadrope and try to get the horse to walk on without pausing, often turning to face the horse at the same time. You cannot get a horse to go anywhere by facing it and pulling. Its automatic reaction is to pull back.

If you are lucky and have made your initial approach correctly, the horse might walk straight into the box alongside you. However, if it does stop, you stop with it, without looking at it or pulling on the rope. Allow it a moment or two to think about things and, if it has stopped at the bottom of the ramp, to sniff at it. The scent of other horses on the ramp may be enough to encourage it in when you again ask it to walk forwards. Do this by taking a step or two forwards yourself and giving a gentle tug and release on the leadrope, still without looking at the horse and without pulling.

The horse may react in a number of ways. It may

enter the box. It may put its front feet on the ramp then stop again, in which case, repeat the above procedure. It may refuse to move, in which case give it a little longer to think about the situation. At this time the horse's attention must be kept on you and the box. Do not allow it to turn away, or even turn its head to look at outside distractions. Eventually, usually within a few minutes the horse will at least step onto the ramp with its front feet. When it does so, rub its face and quietly praise it. The final reaction when you ask the horse to walk on may be that it will go into reverse and pull back. If it does so, go with it and avoid pulling on the leadrope as that will only encourage the horse to pull harder. Lead the horse back to the ramp, preferably without circling away and repeat the above procedure. This may happen several times, with the horse stopping at various points between the foot of the ramp and several feet away.

If this calm, patient approach does not result in

73

the horse walking quietly into the box, you have to assess the situation and decide why the horse is refusing to trust you. There may be a number of reasons as follows.

Lack of travelling experience

The horse may not familiar with travelling and is still too uncertain and wary to accept what you are asking it to do. In this situation, more time and more patience are needed. This is a classic case where opening up the front of the box will help. A bucket of feed may also tempt the horse into the box and, once it is in, allowing it to stand there and eat a few mouthfuls helps the horse get used to standing in the confined space. Eating the food is a displacement activity, which takes the horse's full attention off its own nervousness – rather like a human having a cigarette while waiting for an important appointment. The horse should then be either led through the box or backed quietly out, led around in a circle and asked to repeat the loading procedure, several times, until it walks in without hesitation. This process can be usefully repeated for several days before progressing to putting the ramp up and allowing the horse to stand and eat. Then, after a few more days, it should be ready to go for a short journey.

Challenging the handler

The horse may not be at all frightened and is simply facing you, the handler, with a challenge. Who wins in this situation depends upon your ingenuity and which is the most patient, or the most stubborn – you or the horse. A horse that has been trained to have total respect for its handler does not play this type of game. However, most of us, even with the best of intentions, allow our horses to 'get away with' less than perfect, slightly disrespectful behaviour in various unimportant ways occasionally, because the behaviour is not really inconveniencing us and may even amuse us. The fact that the horse is able to do this encourages it to challenge us in other ways, when it might not be so convenient. We then have two options. We can go back to basics and teach the horse total respect, or we can find a way around the problem.

Going back to basics means using psychology to teach the horse to accept the handler's dominant,

leadership role at all times. This takes considerable time, patience and skill and although it is perfectly possible, as many top trainers have shown, teaching the horse to accept a particular way of coping with a specific situation is enough for most people.

Overcoming the 'stubborn' challenge is not difficult as the horse will remain quite calm unless you, the handler, become excited. In this situation, the 'yard broom' method is unlikely to work as the horse is likely to fight it.

Sometimes, if the horse has stopped at the foot of the ramp, lifting the forefeet one by one and placing them on the ramp will have the effect of encouraging the horse to walk in. It might equally have the effect of the horse just taking them off again, or, if not and if you continue to move the forefeet up, the horse ends up stretched out like a giraffe, refusing to move its hind feet. It is much more difficult to lift the hind feet on to the ramp and, if you are not absolutely certain of your horse's character, you also run a risk of being kicked if you try.

A further development of this method is that once the forefeet are on the ramp, two helpers link arms behind the horse's quarters and, whenever the horse breathes out and relaxes, they push together. It is essential that the person at the front does not pull on the leadrope, otherwise everyone ends up in a tug-of-war, with the horse pulling back and literally sitting on the arms of the helpers at the rear. This method can be successful if the horse is not seriously determined to resist. Big, burly men can manhandle a small horse into a box, but, again, the result is not one of informed horsemanship and the horse will not have learnt the lesson. The whole point is that the horse must decide to give way rather than being forced by the humans. This is why you wait for the horse to breathe out and relax before bringing pressure to bear to encourage it forwards.

Psychologically, we think horses respond more readily to the effect of an inanimate object creating the pressure. You can make up a loading harness – an arrangement of ropes which go around the quarters and through the headcollar rings, so that when the horse pulls back, it encounters the rope around its quarters and is effectively pulling against itself. Alternatively, we clip a lunge line to a piece of string tied to the fixings at the side of the ramp and bring the line around the horse's quarters. After a minute or two of pressure on the lunge line, but keeping the headcollar leadrope slack, the horse will usually walk in. We have one horse now which only has to be shown the lunge line and it will load – without the lunge line, it usually plays the 'stubborn' game. Getting round the problem in this way is indeed a compromise, but for the average owner, who may not have the time or the expertise to teach their horse total respect without fail, it works.

Lack of respect for the handler

In this case the horse is not frightened, but puts up more than just the 'stubborn' challenge. The situation happens with the horse that has not been taught basic good manners and has been allowed to get away with disrespect to an unacceptable extent. This horse barges in the stable, tows its handler around on the leadrope and will not stand still to be attended by the vet or farrier, etc. When you put pressure on, by trying to lift the forefeet on to the ramp, or by encouraging it gently forwards, or attempting to take a lunge line around its quarters, it over-reacts. It will pull back, throw up its head, shake its head violently to try to get rid of the leadrope, twist and turn, try to go to one side or the other of the ramp rather than facing forwards up it, rear, or kick out with its hind legs.

This horse is a nuisance and, while going back to basics and teaching good manners is the only long-term solution, firm handling by the right person will often overcome the problem on a specific occasion. The right person is one who is not impressed by the horse's attempts to intimidate its handlers. They must be capable of moving quickly to block the horse's efforts to escape, must know what will work psychologically with regard to the horse's specific behaviour and be someone whose force of character is such that the horse gives in within a few minutes and not vice versa. If you are the owner and regular handler of such a horse and endure such problems on an ongoing basis, you need expert help to show you how to gain your horse's respect. If you buy a horse and find it behaves in this way, you must find out whether it always behaves in this way, or whether it is just trying you out because you are a

new and unfamiliar person. If the latter, follow the suggestions previously given for handling your horse in hand and become thoroughly familiar with handling it in the simplest ways before you try to travel it anywhere. The time will be well spent. If the former, the horse must be re-trained from basics, or you will never have a happy relationship. In this case, if you are an inexperienced person, get help from a professional – retraining a bad-mannered, badly handled horse is more difficult than starting a youngster and few inexperienced people know what to do quickly enough to stay in charge of the situation. Sometimes, with such horses, it is necessary to be very strongly dominant and administer, not punishment, but strong, fast, determined reactions that show the horse that its behaviour will not succeed in avoiding what it is being asked to do. In this situation, it is all too easy to do the wrong thing, too late!

Real fear

The horse is genuinely frightened, which occurs with horses that, at some time or another, have had a bad experience. Horses like this will often balk at going anywhere near the ramp and will become agitated, even if the handler remains calm. They may twist and turn, try to pull away from the handler, or, if that fails, rear and turn. If they do get as far as having their front feet on the ramp, they may rear up or throw themselves around if asked to go further, or lash out violently if approached with encouragement from behind. This is a potentially dangerous situation and nothing is to be gained from attempting to force the issue.

Such a horse will often behave perfectly well in any other situation, which is another clue to the fact that the horse is genuinely afraid to load.

The key to overcoming the problem, as with any other fear, is to condition or desensitise the horse to its fear by thorough familiarisation with the feared object. Forget completely about going anywhere today – cancel your trip to the show or competition.

There are two ways thereafter to approach the problem, either with the horse in hand or with it loose in an enclosed space from which the only route to food or freedom is via the horsebox or trailer.

The first method, training the horse in hand, involves a great deal of time and patience spent persuading the horse to accept going through increasingly narrower spaces until, finally, it is asked to enter the horsebox. Success depends upon the delicate psychological balance of the horse's fear, the extent to which desensitisation has been successful and the handler's attitude of positive determination without hustling the horse.

The second method may not take any less total time, but it may save you time in that the horse can be left to get on with thinking about the situation without you being permanently on hand. It is also probably the easier and safer option for the non-professional owner.

For the second method, you need a safe enclosed environment, providing shelter for the horse and a small amount of room to wander around. A large, open loosebox, or a shelter opening to a small, enclosed yard area would be ideal. The transport vehicle, ideally a trailer with front and rear ramps, is reversed into the opening gateway and set up safely so that the only way out is via the trailer. Remove the partition and breast bar. Make sure the trailer is supported on blocks if it is not hitched to a towing vehicle in order to prevent tipping when the horse starts to enter. Leave the horse to get used to its new environment. At feeding time, put the food on the ramp, so that the horse will have to put its front feet up in order to reach the food. Each feeding time, move the food progressively further into the trailer. However suspicious a horse is of going in, familiarity does breed contempt and fear of going into the stationary vehicle is usually overcome within a day or two, particularly if the interior is as light as possible. Left to its own devices in this situation the horse also does not feel pressurised by humans trying to persuade it to go in. Do not try to coax the horse to follow you in with the feed, just put it down and leave.

Continue the procedure for a few days so that the horse is thoroughly accustomed to walking up and down the ramp (it will probably turn around inside and walk down, rather than back out) and has learned the lesson that there is no reason to fear the trailer itself. In fact going into the trailer becomes associated with a pleasurable experience – eating dinner!

Once the horse is going in and out freely – you can hang the haynet in the trailer too – it might follow you in for its feed without persuasion. If not, find some odd jobs to do around the yard in the vicinity of the trailer. The next step is to get the horse used to going in and out of the trailer with humans close by and, eventually, for the horse to remain in the trailer to eat when you move right up to the trailer and eventually go in with the horse.

We once had a mare to load that took three weeks to get past this stage. She very quickly went in and out by herself, but as soon as a human ventured within a yard or two of the trailer she shot out again, terrified that the ramp would be shut and she would be taken on a journey. This mare had been severely traumatised by travelling in a cattle truck with slatted sides. Once she finally accepted us in the trailer with her, there was little trouble with the rest of the process and she now travels quite happily.

Once the horse is happy for you to be in the trailer, the next stage is to close the ramp while it eats and then let it down again. Many horses dislike the noise and sensation of the ramp going up behind them in a blind area, so have someone stand at its head and give plenty of reassurance. The person raising the ramp must wear a safety helmet and must be sure to stand to the side of the ramp, not behind it, in case the horse decides to rush out. When the ramp is up, the person inside can leave via the jockey door while the horse is left to eat and think about the situation.

By this time the horse is thoroughly familiar with the trailer and should have discovered that it is not dangerous. Next, the handler should lead the horse into the trailer for its feed and there should be no problem. Once this is achieved, arrange things so that you can lead the horse into the trailer, down the front ramp and back around to the rear with the trailer still in the same location. Ask the horse to walk slowly down the front ramp, one step at a time, but be prepared to move out of the way quickly if necessary as some horses will leap off the ramp. Repeat several times.

The next stage is a short journey. On your return, put the horse back in the loosebox or enclosed area and set the trailer up as before. Feed the horse in the trailer. If the horse shows any signs of nervousness, repeat this exercise several times, so that the horse is still exposed to the trailer after travelling and can re-establish in its mind that there is nothing to fear.

The final step is to move the trailer and load the horse in a different location. Make the set up as easy as possible for the horse and lead it into the trailer, with food if necessary, exactly as you did from the loosebox. Provided each stage has been carried out with patience, sufficient repetition and not until the horse is ready to progress further, there should be no further difficulties.

This may seem a long-winded way around a problem, but it has the advantage of being thorough and gives you the confidence of knowing that you have given the horse every opportunity to develop confidence and trust in you whilst overcoming its fear. How long it takes and how effectively it works depends to a degree upon the temperament of the horse, but once the horse is confidently going in and out for food and accepting the ramp being closed, any past fear has really been overcome. Refusal to load thereafter can be put down to other reasons, such as disrespect, as discussed earlier.

Once you have taken the trouble to do all this, it is very important to ensure that the horse is given a good ride by careful and considerate driving when being transported, or you may quickly find yourself back to square one.

Unloading

Unloading seldom presents a problem when the horse can be led forwards down the ramp so that it can see where it is going. However, an individual horse will sometimes dislike unloading backwards and this problem needs to be overcome to prevent the risk of injury. The ideal solution is to avoid the situation by using a trailer with a front ramp and leading the horse out. If this is not possible, try to park with the trailer facing slightly down hill so that the ramp slopes as little as possible when lowered. It is usually the feeling of the downward slope of the ramp that panics the horse. Try to persuade the horse to move back slowly, one step at a time, but be prepared for a rush. If the horse does rush back,

Hitching a ride! The calm attitude of well cared for horses making a long journey together shows that the whole travelling experience is nothing to worry about.

Unloading at a rest stop, the broom and shovel are ready to remove droppings from the transporter.

quickly release the leadrope (it is not a bad idea to attach a lunge line to the headcollar before unloading, to give you extra length). If you try to hang on, the horse is more likely to throw up its head and risk hitting it on the roof of the trailer. Take some time to practise unloading at home.

Travelling problems

Some horses find it difficult to stay upright within the confines of their travelling space, particularly in trailers with full-height, solid partitions, which do not allow the horse to spread its feet sufficiently far to balance themselves. Replacing the partition with one with a moveable rubber sheet, or removing it altogether will often solve this problem. Do not, however, remove the breast bar – this is essential to give the horse support when the vehicle brakes.

In Britain, where driving is on the left-hand side of the road, horses travel best on the right-hand side of the trailer. If transporting one horse in a double trailer, always put it on the right-hand side, where the effect of centrifugal force, when the vehicle goes around bends is minimised. Some horses find it very difficult to adapt to travelling on the left and may always need to be on the right. Most horses will travel happily with a companion. However, some

panic if another horse is in such close proximity in a trailer and those are best transported alone.

Lorries have many different partition arrangements – forward or backward facing, sideways or herringbone pattern, depending on the size and design of the lorry. The ride in a lorry is generally more stable than in a trailer and most horses travel happily enough.

Travelling care

Finally, it is important for the health of the horse that the travelling compartment is kept clean. On long journeys, remove droppings and wet bedding at every rest stop. Ideally, horses should not travel more than four hours at a time without a break to rest and stretch their legs. At the same time offer a drink and let them graze or have a small, wet feed.

Horses lose a considerable amount of bodyweight while travelling, most of which comprises water and essential salts. It is therefore vital to make sure a horse is well hydrated before setting out on a long journey. Giving electrolytes in the feed for a couple of days before the trip can assist with this, provided the horse is eating and drinking normally and well.

Chapter 6

Basic Riding

Some people keep horses just to look at, some perhaps for the pleasure of watching their horses compete while others ride, but most owners keep one or two horses to ride for their own pleasure, be it competitively or hacking out. New parents often speak of the shock of discovering that the new member of the family is not just a beautiful, compliant adjunct of themselves, but a fully independent being with behaviour, demands, thoughts and needs which are all its own and frequently not in accord with its parents! A new horse can bring much the same shocking revelation.

Mounting

We have discussed tacking up in Chapter 4. The next step is to mount. A well-schooled horse should stand still to be mounted. Whether it should stand still to be mounted by someone who digs a toe into its ribs whilst hauling themselves up by hanging on to the reins with one hand and the back of the saddle with the other is another matter entirely. Ideally, all riders should be fit, athletic people, but we cannot all conform to an ideal and many of us have lost the spring and resilience of youth, or may have some minor disability that prevents us from emulating Mark

Tammy stands square for Becky to mount, but she is eager to be off, as her tension and slightly raised tail show.

Becky mounts carefully (note her toe turned away from the horse's side), but Tammy's head comes up and she takes a step forward in anticipation.

As she reaches the saddle, Becky asks her to stand. Tammy's tail swishing shows her reluctance to obey. When teaching a horse to stand to be mounted, it is essential to stay calm, quiet and be precise with your handling.

Todd. Therefore, if mounting from the ground presents you with a difficulty, be practical and use a mounting block. It is not a bad idea anyway, when the horse is first saddled and before the girth is fully tightened, to mount from a block. You will avoid the risk of the saddle slipping round too far and a potential fall, as well as the discomfort caused to the horse by weight dragging down one side of the saddle.

The obvious solution for a horse that experiences discomfort when being mounted is to move off. A horse that is fresh, keen and eager may also do this. Some start to move as soon as they first feel your weight in the stirrup, leaving you dangling in an undignified manner if you are not quick enough to spring up from your foot on the ground! Nasty accidents can occur if a horse takes off leaving a rider unbalanced with one foot caught in the stirrup, so it is well worth organising yourself to mount safely.

A mounting block can be anything from a low wall to an upturned tub or a specially built arrangement of steps and platform. The bumper of a vehicle or the ramp of a lorry will do at times. However, if the horse is inclined to move off, set up a solid mounting block that is safe and secure for you to stand on.

Provided the horse is well schooled, comfortable and willing to stand still, mounting from a block presents no problems.

The procedure is as follows:

- **Lead the horse alongside the mounting block and step up to the platform. Take up the reins evenly (in your left hand if mounting from the left side and vice versa).**
- **Steady the stirrup and step into it with your toe facing forwards. As you are already at a height where you can balance in the stirrup without having to spring up, all you have to do if the horse should chance to move off is to swing your right leg over and settle in the saddle.**
- **Place your right hand on the pommel of the saddle, take your weight on it and on the foot**

in the stirrup and balance yourself momentarily.

- **Lean forwards, raise your other leg, taking care to keep it straight, and lift it clear over the horse's back.**
- **Settle softly into the saddle and turn the outside stirrup leather so that you can slip your foot in easily without disturbing the horse.**
- **If your seat is secure and the horse well trained, you can simply turn your toe inwards to find your outside stirrup; if you are a novice, be careful not to dig the horse in the ribs.**

Traditions differ as to the merits of facing forwards or backwards when mounting and as to the risk of falling if the horse moves off in the process. British tradition dictates that it is easier to complete the mounting process safely if you start facing the rear of the horse, but techniques in other countries for mounting standing or moving horses indicate no proof either way.

To mount from the left:

- **Take the reins in your left hand, with the outside rein fractionally shorter than the inside rein. Then, if the horse begins to move, it will turn its quarters towards you, making it easier to complete the mounting action and minimising the risk of a fall.**
- **Put your hand on the neck in front of the withers and face the rear.**
- **With your right hand, turn the back of the stirrup outwards and, raising your left knee, place your left foot in the stirrup, close to the horse's side.**
- **Spring up, straightening your left knee and support yourself lightly with your right hand on the waist of the saddle. Never pull yourself up holding on to the cantle as you risk damaging the saddle tree by twisting it. If holding on is essential, reach forwards to the back of the outside flap.**
- **Take care to point your toe down under the horse's belly as you turn.**
- **Lean forwards and swing your leg over as before, then settle gently into the saddle.**

The 'leg up' is a way of mounting without the need to use stirrups or a mounting block. It is mostly employed by jockeys, who ride with stirrups too short to be reached from the ground. Racehorses are also often too lively and full of oats to stand still and an athletic jockey can be legged up onto a horse that is dancing on the spot or going round in circles! For the less athletic rider, it is an alternative when no mounting block is available but helpers are to hand. The horse must be relied on to stand quietly, or be held. The rider takes up the reins in the usual way, and stands facing the left

A low wall can serve as a mounting block.

81

side of the horse with their left leg raised and bent at the knee. The helper giving the leg up supports the rider's knee in their left hand and ankle in their right hand. Rider and helper must have agreed a signal on which the rider springs and the helper lifts. The rider must take care to swing their leg clear of the horse's back as the momentum carries them up and over. The timing takes practice: too little lift and the rider is left struggling up the horse's side; too much and they may well land on the other side of the horse.

Vaulting on to the horse is another mounting option. If you are strong, fit and athletic enough, vaulting on causes very little disturbance to the horse – otherwise, do not even attempt it. The ability to vault on may also be useful if you want to mount a moving horse, as endurance riders who dismount and run alongside their horses often do when they want to remount. A certain amount of momentum is needed to vault on, so you must be able to time your movements to the horse's movement or potential movement. To vault on you need to be able to spring upwards high enough for your hands to be able to support your weight briefly while you swing your leg clear of the horse's back.

If the horse has learned to associate being mounted with discomfort, you need to show it that there is nothing to fear. Short-term solutions include having a helper hold the horse while you mount, or standing it facing a corner, so that there is nowhere for it to go when it tries to move. These remedies will not solve the problem long term, however, unless you also take the time to re-educate the horse. This should be done in the same way that a young horse is trained to accept the saddle and to be backed (see Chapter 11).

A horse which reacts violently to being mounted, for example, by rearing, going down on its knees, or bucking when asked to move off, is almost certainly suffering pain for some reason and the cause needs to be investigated before further attempts are made to ride the animal (see Chapter 12).

Dismounting

The dismounting procedure is as follows:

- **After work, the horse should be asked to halt square, with its weight evenly balanced on all four feet.**
- **Stroke or rub the horse's neck and talk to it, releasing the reins so that the horse can stretch its head and neck and relax.**
- **Lightly take up the reins again so that you have enough control if the horse decides to move.**
- **Slip both feet out of the stirrups, place your right hand on the pommel, lean forward and, straightening your outside leg, swing it clear over the horse's back.**
- **Support yourself momentarily on your hands, then drop lightly down, turning towards the front of the horse as you do so and bending your knees slightly for balance as you land. You turn towards the front so that you can move in the right direction if the horse begins to walk off.**
- **Take the reins over the horse's head and hang the buckle ends over your arm while you loosen the girth one or two holes and put up the stirrups. Loosening the girth makes the horse comfortable and helps it relax, whilst also gradually releasing any pressure from the saddle on its back. Dangling stirrup irons can be dangerous – they may bang against the horse's side and worry it should it make any sudden movement, become caught up in a gate, or even cause an injury if the horse gets loose, or falls.**

It is not advisable to dismount leaving one foot in the stirrup. If the horse moves off, you are likely to fall backwards before you can release your foot. Swinging one leg over the horse's neck to dismount is equally dangerous, again if the horse moves off, or if, as is very likely when it is surprised in this way, it throws its head up and catches your leg before it is safely over.

If your horse stands quietly to be mounted and dismounted always remember to caress and praise it for its good behaviour. This helps reinforce desired behaviour patterns even in older and well-trained horses. The training of a horse and your relationship with it is never finished business. Everything you do with your horse today will be reflected in the way it behaves tomorrow.

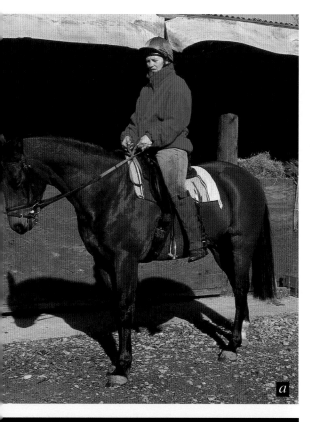

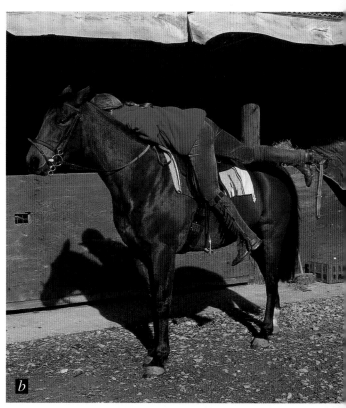

a) To dismount, Becky keeps a light contact in halt and takes both feet from the stirrups.

b) She leans forward and swings her leg clear of the saddle.

c) As she lands, she turns to face forwards in case the horse moves off and flexes her knees to absorb concussion and keep her balance.

Communicating with the horse from the saddle

This section is not going tell you how to ride by describing the way you get the horse to move, stop and steer. Unfortunately that is what many riding instructors do, particularly those who never progress past the basic levels of riding themselves. They will tell you what to do with your hands and legs and explain that you must have an 'independent seat', which they will endeavour to teach you by making you trot round the manege for hours without stirrups.

Frankly, you can do this for the rest of your life *but if you do not understand and absorb how the different parts of your body should feel*, both individually and in unison, you will never have that vital 'independent seat'. It is completely useless to *know what* to do, if you cannot *feel how* to do it. Methods such as Centred Riding, developed by Sally Swift and the Alexander Technique (see Further Reading list) can help tremendously with this process, which is based on awareness of what happens in your own body in conjunction with what happens in the body of the horse.

What is an independent seat? It is a way of sitting on a horse so that your upper body, from your head through your spine, is balanced over your seat bones, with your pelvis vertical whether the horse is standing still or moving. With your upper body balanced, your lower body (i.e., your legs, beginning most importantly with your hip joints) can be free of tension and able to work effectively to control and guide the horse. Similarly, your hands and arms are yours to control and no part of your body is tense, clutching, or gripping up. If any part of you is tense or gripping, the horse will tense itself against the discomfort this causes, making your efforts to ride or control it ineffective. The 'independent' seat is so-called because your body, supported by your seat, is balanced on the horse independently of the need for assistance from your hands, arms and legs. If the latter were cut off, you would not fall off.

We are going to look at riding in terms of layers, like the layers of a birthday cake, which can be built up to enable you to enjoy an effective relationship with your horse from the saddle:

- **The cake base, or your position and body alignment on the stationary horse.**
- **The almond paste, or your position and body alignment on the moving horse.**
- **The icing, or the co-ordination of your body movements (aids) with those of the horse.**

The cake base – position on the standing horse

As children, we were taught 'position', as many riding schools still do, in the following way: sit up straight, keep your shoulders back, keep your elbows in, keep your knees in, point your toe forwards and keep your heels down. Not a word was said in those unenlightened days of the need to keep on breathing, or to avoid tension!

If you refer back to Chapter 1, you will remember we said that fear was the greatest obstacle in the way of success in handling and riding horses. For most people who have not grown up with horses, getting on for the first time can be quite a nerve-wracking business. When you first begin to ride, whether on your own or in a lesson, if steps are not taken straight away to overcome that nervousness and fear, you are likely to continue to be tense and nervous, to a greater or lesser degree, every time you mount a horse.

Nervousness often becomes worse when an instructor starts to give you directions of the 'Do this, do not do that' variety. Such instructions have to be followed by means of conscious thought. For example, the instructor says, 'Sit up!' so you think about it and then do it. But what exactly do you do? How do you convert the instruction 'Sit up!' into a physical movement?

Some people might stretch vigorously upwards, chin up, chest thrust out and shoulders back. Others might think they are obeying but be so inhibited they hardly move at all. It is not difficult to see that instruction on this basis lacks understanding, let alone effectiveness.

The first person might have obeyed the instruction, but are they now sitting in strained stiffness, with a hollow back and holding their breath? The second person may incur the instructor's wrath: 'I said "Sit up straight!"' Yet when you are mesmerised with fear, the instinctive human reaction is to curl up in a ball. This is difficult on a horse, but you can hunch your shoulders, collapse your ribs and clutch the reins to your stomach pretty effectively! At the same time your hips will be tensely blocked so that anything you try to do with your legs will be totally disconnected from your upper body.

Many people decide to learn to ride without taking the time to accustom themselves to horses first. Riding schools compound this error in the belief that the client is anxious to get on a horse and gallop and jump, so they do not spend time teaching people how to behave around horses and handle them in a confident, practical, understanding way. Often, riding school staff themselves are short of time and the horses either have to conform to a way of life, or be 'misfits' who are eventually sold on.

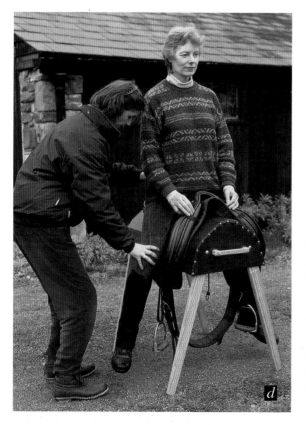

d) The Alexander Technique is one method of improving your riding. Alexander teacher Sally Tottle adjusts a student's position using the 'wooden horse'.

e) To maintain balance, the rider must sit straight and symetrically in the saddle.

f) Riding on the lunge helps to improve the rider's seat.

If, before you start to ride, or try to ride, you get used to handling horses and playing 'games' with them on the ground, as described in the previous chapters, then confidence and effectiveness in the saddle will be easier to attain. You will already have discovered much about how horses react to different stimuli, how they move and how to interpret their behaviour.

Let us assume you have a well-schooled horse, which is used to being ridden. You have mounted safely and the horse is standing still in a safe, clear space, waiting for your instructions.

You will not be involved with horses and riding for long before you hear the term 'feel'. Top riders

ABOVE: *The upper arms should hang vertically, with the elbows bent and the hands carried lightly with thumbs uppermost,*

RIGHT: *Adjusting the leg position. Sally helps the rider to obtain the correct 'feel'.*

use this word to describe how they achieve what they do. 'You have a "feel" for it or you do not,' is a common expression, often with the implication that 'feel' is something mysterious, which is denied to the majority of us lesser riders. This is nonsense, but effective riding is all about feel and perception and very little about consciously thinking and doing. So the first thing you are going to do is enable yourself to discover a 'feel' for riding.

Tension destroys our ability to do the simplest things. Pick up any small object and put it back down in a specified spot, then try to do the same gripping with a tense arm and hand. Notice how much more effort it takes and how the sensitivity of your movement is reduced.

If you are worried about the horse moving off, have someone hold it so that your attention is not distracted while you concentrate on feeling your way to a good position.

Release your stirrups and let your arms hang naturally by your sides. Without attempting to change anything, consider your body and the position you have automatically taken up. Notice if you are sitting on your seat bones and whether your weight is even on each one. Is there any tension in your head, neck, shoulders, ribcage, arms, elbows, wrists, pelvis, hips, thighs, knees, calves, ankles? Where are your eyes focused? Are you breathing naturally, or holding your breath?

Wherever tensions exist, now is the time to get rid of them. First, let your eyes soften. Be aware of your surroundings peripherally, without focusing on one specific thing. This will help to turn your attention inward and to release tensions in your head and neck.

Next, think of your breathing. Let your ribcage expand and fill up naturally with air, right to the bottom of your lungs. Most of us restrict our air intake by collapsing our waist and hunching our shoulders, or forcing them back and down.

Breathing naturally will help you to avoid tipping forwards at the waist, a very common fault, which completely unbalances your body. At this point, a conventional instructor might say, 'Do not lean forwards.' You might then make all kinds of efforts to obey, none of them effective. Instead, allow yourself to feel the air filling up your lungs and let your ribcage rise to accommodate it.

Now think of your head, which you have no doubt frequently been told is very heavy. You may have been told to hold it up, but this is not really the answer. The solution is to hold it balanced. The pivotal point where your head is connected to your spine lies between the hollows immediately behind your earlobes and it is from this point that you can balance your head. If you stretch up with your chin out, the weight of your head overbalances backwards. If you look down with your chin tucked in, your head overbalances forwards. Try to feel the point where your head is perfectly balanced and upright – for most people it is necessary to drop the chin a little further than initially feels comfortable. Continue to breathe and allow any tension to flow out of your shoulders, upper arms and elbows.

Your seat is your main point of contact with the horse, bearing the weight of your upper body. The effect of this weight is minimised if it is carried in a balanced way. Without collapsing your ribcage, put your hands under your seatbones and feel what your horse's back feels when you sit on it. Let the muscles of your buttocks soften and as an experiment move your weight first over one seatbone, then the other. Your seatbones, aided by the soft muscles of your buttocks, support the weight of your upper body transferred down from your head, through your spine to your pelvis. Imagine your seatbones as a set of balance scales. If the weight above tips one way or another, due to one side of your body collapsing, or your head moving out of balance with its pivotal joint to the top of your spine, the scales will tip to one side or another, or backwards or forwards. When you feel the weight evenly over each hand, remove your hands.

As every rider knows, their back should be straight. Nature, however, did not take this into account when designing the human body and made the spine up of a series of gentle curves! If you consciously try to straighten your back, the natural balance of these curves will become distorted and you will tip too much weight either backwards or forwards. A naturally balanced posture of the upper body as described above, however, will allow the spine to lengthen, without tension and become a strong, supple and flexible support for your upper body.

Many instructors teach clients to 'brace the back' to drive the horse forwards, and the poor rider then wonders why their horse puts its nose in the air and hollows its back. Meanwhile the instructor is busy telling them to 'get the horse on the bit'. Bracing the back means stiffening the back to most people and this causes the seatbones to jar the horse's back, making it uncomfortable, so, of course, it hollows in the attempt to get away from the discomfort. A nervous, tense rider may unwittingly cause the same effect. Correct use of the back muscles comes later in learning riding techniques, but for now all you need to know is that your back should be free of stiffness and allowed to assume its full natural length, so that it can absorb the movement of the horse.

Also within your pelvis are your hip joints, another part of the body that causes unwitting frustration to the novice rider. Your hip joints are not the coat hangers on which skinny models hang designer clothes, but are lower down and further in. In the lower pelvis is the socket into which the ball of the hip joint is inserted. The ball is at the end of an angled offshoot of the top of your thighbone, or femur. When standing on the ground, you can find your hip joint by raising and lowering your knee and feeling for it with your fingers. The length of the offshoot from the hip joint to thighbone allows more space for the rider's seat and legs to fit round the horse.

If you are nervous when you get on a horse it is almost an automatic response to tense your hips and legs. Your body is telling you 'get ready to jump!' It is a natural reaction in anticipation of having to get out of harm's way. Unfortunately, unless your hips are free and open, they cannot absorb the separate movements of each side of the horse, your legs cannot act independently and effectively and your upper and lower body cannot work in harmony.

Allow your legs to hang naturally by your horse's sides, remaining aware of being equally balanced on your seatbones. Allow your buttocks again to soften and let your legs become heavy.

Provided the horse is well behaved, allow first one leg, then the other, to swing gently backwards and forwards, so that you can feel the location of your hip joints and allow the tension to release.

Many people have tense, or 'blocked' hips, through habitually poor body use or simply lack of use of the full range of movement, which is considerable, as watching any accomplished dancer will reveal. Allowing them to become completely free may take some time and perseverance, but is well worth the effort.

Blocked hips are usually accompanied by tension through the rest of the leg. Allow your thigh muscles to soften, both inner and outer. Let your knees drop downward, lying flat against the saddle without gripping. Be aware of tension in your calves, shins and ankles and let it flow away. Finally, flex your heels just enough to regain your stirrups. You may find that they feel too short.

Extraordinarily, if you have followed each stage of aligning, balancing and freeing your body as outlined above, you should now be in a riding position that any instructor would be proud of! Maintaining and refining it will take some time and you will need to repeat the process continually until your body remembers the right 'feel' and adopts it automatically. However, it *will* happen and once your body is correctly aligned and balanced, you can move on to the next stage, which is to maintain balance on the moving horse.

The almond paste – maintaining body alignment on the moving horse

Riding is like dancing with a partner. Every small movement of the individual parts of your body must be co-ordinated with each other and with those of the horse in order to obtain a harmonious and pleasurable relationship. This is achieved through allowing yourself to feel your way to the right movements, not through consciously trying to move the various parts of your body in a particular way. Harmonious co-ordination is impossible unless your body is in balance with itself and the horse.

Without losing the position you have discovered above, take up your reins to a light contact with the bit and ask the horse to walk forwards. Ideally, have someone lead the horse, or lunge you, so that you can concentrate on the feel of your body in conjunction with that of the horse.

The aim now is to become accustomed to the feeling of the way the horse moves underneath you, without trying to influence it in any way. That comes later. Remind yourself to breathe and allow your lungs to fill with air, letting your ribcage lift and expand. Keep the focus of your eyes soft with your attention on yourself and on what you feel *right now*. Forget about cooking supper, or taking the kids to football – do not even let your mind wander to whether you remembered to put the horse's brushing boots on. Allow your upper body to remain in balance as the horse takes each step. Feel each stride *as it happens*. The previous stride is in the past and you cannot do anything about it; the next is still in the future and will be good if the present one is good.

As each hind leg comes to the ground, the horse's belly on that side will swing towards your leg. As the horse takes its weight on that leg, his back on that side will rise under you. Note how it feels. As the hind leg lifts off the ground and swings forwards the horse's back will dip on that side and your seatbone will feel as though it is sinking and sliding forwards. Do not consciously try to repeat this movement with your body; if you do the two will get out of synchronisation and your body will look as though it is moving too much on the horse, instead of being still – remember the great riders never appear to move in the saddle. Simply allow the horse to move under you and allow your hips and seat the freedom to be a part of that movement. Good riding position and balance is all about allowing the movement of the horse to initiate movements in your body without you losing your posture through tension, reverting to gripping, or blocking the horse's movement unconsciously – especially through the hips. If you sit correctly, in balance, the horse will eventually discover that it is easier to move correctly, in balance and this leads to harmony. If a less experienced rider continually tries to make corrections to the horse's way of going the usual result is over-reaction, with neither horse nor rider able to find and maintain balance.

You will have read or been told that the rhythm of the walk is four-time: right hind, right fore, left hind, left fore. If the rider is unbalanced, the smooth rhythm of the pace is often disturbed. As you continue to practise maintaining position and balance

whilst absorbing the movement, notice whether your horse is moving rhythmically with four equal beats to its walk. If not, check that you are sitting quietly and not anticipating the horse's action by moving your seatbones yourself; check your breathing and check for tension through your head, neck, back and hips. If necessary, halt and begin again.

It is well worth spending a good deal of time working in walk and practising simple balance and body alignment. It will pay huge dividends in everything else you try to do with your horse from the saddle, from riding a dressage test to enjoying a hack in the country, to coping with any problems.

Learning to trot can be a major problem for the novice rider. You are told that the trot is a diagonal two-time pace: left hind and right fore together, followed by right hind and left fore. You may be told to count one, two, one, two, as you trot and to rise on the 'one' and sit on the 'two'.

At varying times and by different instructors, I have been told 'Emphasise the rise and let yourself drop softly back into the saddle'; 'Concentrate on the sit and let the horse throw you naturally into the rise'; 'Push your waist forwards as you rise'; and 'Do not rise from the saddle more than necessary'. As you can see from this list, there are some conflicting ideas

LEFT: *The horse in walk: The sequence of footfalls here is right hind, right fore, left hind, left fore.*

BELOW: *In trot, the diagonal pairs strike the ground in turn.*

about on how the trot should be taught or performed. Particularly horrendous is the instructor who insists that you do rising trot without stirrups!

The trot is faster than the walk, a fact which immediately causes tension in the beginner, which they may be unable to dispel without help, particularly if the basics of balance and an independent seat have not been fully developed first.

The horse's back also moves up and down a lot more in trot than in walk, so there is a great deal more motion which the rider's balanced body must allow for. Frequently, the rider does not make sufficient allowance and thus becomes unbalanced. In trying to maintain or recover balance they tense up, grip and stiffen, which in turn makes the horse uncomfortable and causes it to lose its rhythm and either break gait, or run on, falling on the forehand.

Theories vary as to whether the sitting or rising trot should be taught first. The rising trot is often thought to be 'easier', but this is just because any faults do not cause the rider to lose control quite so quickly.

In the trot, the horse's legs move in diagonal pairs, with a moment of suspension in between. As each diagonal pair strike the ground the horse's body sinks. As they spring up to the moment of suspension, the horse's body rises. As the legs move in diagonal pairs, there will also be a side to side feel to the movement. In sitting trot, as in the walk, your hip joints must be open and free to follow the horse's body down, then let it rise up under you again. Sitting trot is often practised without stirrups to prevent the rider from trying to counteract the horse's movement by using the stirrups for support. However, when the hips, knees and ankles are free from tension, they will flex and give naturally in co-ordination with the feet in the stirrups. Your ability to sit to the trot is a good test of whether or not you have fully appreciated the feel of opening and freeing your hips.

It is also a common and natural tendency to tense and stiffen the back, shoulders and arms in an effort to counteract the speed and unbalancing effect of the transition to trot. Tensing your muscles prepares them for evasive action – the old 'Get ready to jump!' syndrome – but you must inhibit this natural response by making your body wait for the horse's movement and then allowing it to cause your body to move – not the other way around. Remember to breathe and let your upper body grow, while maintaining the feel of balance that you developed in walk. Your lower back is then able to absorb some of the horse's movement through the flexibility allowed by the correct alignment of your spine and pelvis.

When you first start to trot, do not be too ambitious. Trot a few strides and then ride forwards into walk. Do this by letting your upper body grow, your lower body stretch down and think, 'walk'. When you have a good quality walk, trot a few more strides. Repeat the process until you are comfortable with the trot.

Many people make the mistake, when learning rising trot, of using their stirrups as a springboard to launch them into the rise. It is the movement of the horse that precipitates the rider's seat from the saddle – the rider does not need to help! Sit quietly and feel whether your feet are evenly balanced in the stirrups, at the same time allow your legs to hang with their full weight down the horse's sides. Check whether you are putting more weight on one side of your foot than the other and whether your toes are curled and stiff or relaxed and evenly spread in your boot. Let your ankles and knees act as shock absorbers, not as pistons.

Another mistake is to lean too far forwards, sometimes collapsing the waist as well. As you let the rhythm of the horse carry you forwards, remember to breathe to the bottom of your lungs. As the thrust of the horse's inside hind leg lifts your seat from the saddle, let the front of your body come forwards and up. Allow your weight to rest evenly on the stirrups without pushing against them and let your joints open and close with the flow of the movement, without exaggerating it in any way. Notice the rhythm of the horse's movement and whether or not it is a regular 'one, two'. If not, either there is a physical reason, such as back pain or lameness, or your position is causing the horse to become unbalanced. The latter is the more usual reason!

In canter, which has a three-time beat, the horse's back rises through the moment of suspension as it brings its hind legs forwards ready to strike off with the outside hind, moves forwards as the opposite diagonal pair take the weight and then sinks down in front as the inside leading leg comes to the ground. The motion is one of tipping forwards and back and is absorbed by opening and closing your hip joints

In canter, the outside hind is about to strike off to begin the stride, followed by the opposite diagonal pair and, finally, the inside fore, called the leading leg. The horse's back rises in front as it prepares to strike off.

Now the horse's back dips at the front as the hind legs come through, ready to begin the next canter stride.

in time with the movement while keeping your seat soft and deep. It may surprise you how much movement of your hip joints the canter requires and how slow the movement feels once you have mastered it. Take care not to shorten the horse's stride and unbalance him by leaning forwards in anticipation of each downward movement. Wait for the horse to take you there, keeping your upper body balanced and free.

The icing – the co-ordination of your body movements with those of the horse

Now it begins to become more difficult, mainly because most riders do far too much, moving not only hands and lower legs, but also arms, shoulders and the whole upper body in the effort to 'follow' the movement of the horse.

The basic thing to remember is that you can only influence your horse effectively from a perfectly balanced position. If you try to do so when you are not in perfect balance, your aids will have an exaggerated, or confusing, or totally different effect from what you wanted. The horse will over-react, or react differently from the way you expected, or in extreme cases will back off and refuse to co-operate at all, perhaps napping or bucking. This is usually the cue for the unenlightened rider to punish the horse!

When you are well balanced and in tune with your horse, it takes only a slight movement – an adjustment of your seat, turn of the hips, nudge or squeeze with the lower leg, sponging squeeze on a rein – to produce a response from the well-schooled horse.

To ride effectively, you must ride in the present, not hour by hour, or even exercise by exercise, but stride by stride. A horse can only change where it is going with its legs when the leg in question leaves the ground. Therefore to give an effective aid, you must know when the horse's leg is about to leave the ground and give it the appropriate cue. To do this, your body must be able to feel the movement of each leg through your seat via the horse's back. When you are balanced, the horse moves rhythmically, so this is not as complicated as it sounds. For example, when the horse is in walk, as its right hind leg carries its body forwards, you will feel its back rising on that side and its belly will swing outward towards your right leg. This is the opportune moment to use your right leg to ask the horse to continue forwards, bend, increase impulsion, etc. As the four-time stride sequence continues, the left hind leg contacts the ground on the third beat, the horse's belly swings left and you can use your left leg.

The same theory applies throughout your riding and it does not matter whether you are in an arena, or out for a hack – your horse will be happier and go better for you, if you are in balance. Fortunately, when you have overcome your body's initial and, in many respects, quite natural blocks to balanced riding, it becomes easier to rediscover your balanced, independent seat each time you ride.

Many people, when starting to ride for the first time, focus a great amount of attention on their hands. They have heard that their hands must be light, sympathetic, quiet and not jar the horse's mouth, yet just looking at them and thinking about them encourages an increase of tension. At the same time, they psychologically liken their hands and reins to the steering wheel of a car. It seems obvious that pulling the rein one way or another will steer the horse and pulling back will make it stop. Many people spend the rest of their riding careers trying to reconcile this automatic tendency with the conflicting advice they have been given about sympathetic hands. Once again, it appears, only the expert, gifted by God, can have the blessing of 'light hands'. For the rest of us, this key to perfect riding must remain an unattainable mystery.

As with the other 'mysteries' of effective horsemanship, this is nonsense. The key, again, is in the independent seat (which I hope, having read the above, you no longer consider a mystery) and in your ability to allow the impetus of the horse's movement to continue to flow through your open, relaxed hips, flexible knees and ankles, and soft buttocks and lower back.

If you achieve this, while maintaining the balance of your head, neck and spine, then you can release any tension in your shoulders and they will remain still in relation to the forward movement of the horse. If your shoulders are not bobbing about all over the place, you can control what your upper arm, elbow, lower arm, wrists and hands do. If you have to tense up your arms in the attempt to keep them steady, the problem comes back to your seat and invariably will be found to lie in blocked hips and a stiff lower back. A horse can only respond to any aid if it understands that it is being given one. It can only understand that if it can distinguish the aid from any other movements the rider may make. That is only possible when the rider is balanced with their body toned and supported but not tense, as a stiff, unbalanced rider continually and unwittingly gives a whole range of meaningless, jumbled signals to the horse.

Let us assume you have sorted out your seat and are riding in balance. The first thing to do is get rid of the conception of your hands and reins as a means of steering. If a horse does have a steering wheel, it is controlled by your legs and weight rather than your hands! Think of your hands instead as a means of receiving, conducting and distributing the energy that is produced by the power of the horse's hind quarters. Imagine the reins as conductors of a current of energy, or a flow of life's blood from your hands to the horse's mouth and treat them with as much respect as if they were.

Dedicated trainers, such as Pat Parelli and Shuna Mardon have proved that it is perfectly possible to ride a horse in balance, in all kinds of activities, with no bridle at all. It should not be so difficult, therefore, to learn how to use the reins as an aid rather than a crutch.

We have already established how much more difficult it is to control hand and arm when they are tense. The same freedom that is needed in your leg joints is needed in the joints of your arms – shoulders, elbows, wrists and finger joints. A common fault of beginners is to hunch the shoulders and ride with stiff, blocked elbows. They have been told 'Keep your shoulders still and your elbows close to your sides.'

As already mentioned, if you are in balanced movement, your shoulders will take care of themselves. You need to let the tension run out of them and down your upper arms, which should hang naturally down your sides, not clutched inwards to your ribs. Next, let the tension drop out of the back of your elbows. Imagine a piece of elastic connecting your ring fingers, along the outside of your lower arm to the elbow, up the back of your upper arm to your armpits and then into your back muscles. Feel the co-ordination of the horse's movements through your seat and back, along this piece of elastic and into your receiving hands.

The horse, as we know, uses its head and neck to balance itself and this involves considerable movement of the head and neck in relation to the rest of its body, so that, in walk especially, the horse raises and lowers its head and neck. Your hands, as you will have been told, have to follow this movement. Many beginners are so worried about jarring the horse's mouth that they attempt to anticipate the movement, pushing their hands forwards and losing contact altogether on the down beat and pulling their hands up and back towards their chest on the up beat.

Think of the position of your hands and arms on the stationary horse, with a straight line from your elbow, along your lower arm, wrist, hand and rein to the horse's mouth. As the horse moves forwards, it stretches its neck forwards and down. To follow the movement, it is necessary to open your elbow and shoulder joints, which will also take your hands forwards, following the horse's stretch. At mid-stride, the horse's head comes back up and all your hands have to do is return to where they started, closing the elbow and shoulder joints as you go. In this way you can keep a light, flexible contact.

What about the position of your hands? First of all, let us be clear that we are talking about their position in relation to your arms and not in relation to the horse. There is in fact only one position from which your hands can collect the energy that flows up through the horse's back from its quarters and exert an effective influence on the speed, power and direction with which it continues forwards.

With your upper arms hanging straight and softly down your body, bend your elbows. Your lower arms will rise, coming slightly inwards towards the centre of your body, as they would if you were doing any task with your hands. Look at your hands. Provided you did not consciously turn them when you bent your elbows, it is likely that they are already in the position needed for riding, that is, with the wrists straight and your thumbs uppermost. In this position, the bones of your lower arm lie parallel, allowing freedom and sensitivity when you use your hands. If you turn your hands with the thumbs inwards and knuckles uppermost, the forearm bones cross each other, stiffening your wrist.

Drop your lower arms to relax them and then bend your elbows again, this time being sure to let your thumbs be uppermost. Let the tension out of your elbows whilst keeping them bent and feel the slight effort needed from your forearm muscles to keep your hands raised. This is 'carrying' your hands – another expression you may have heard and a very important one. Only if you take responsibility for carrying your own hands can you use the reins to communicate with the horse with any hope of it understanding what you want.

Now consider your fingers. When you raise your hands, as directed, letting your fingers take care of themselves, your knuckles will be vertical and your fingers probably more or less open. Beginning with the little fingers, gently close them until the pads of each finger are touching the palm of your hand. If you glance down, you should be able to see your fingernails obliquely. Bend your thumbs slightly so that the pad

rests on top of the index finger.

At this point, the frequently used image of holding a baby bird in each hand is useful to describe the small amount of tension which should normally be in your hand when holding the rein. A light squeeze to increase this pressure, as though squeezing water from a sponge, gives a light rein aid. Rotating the wrist slightly, so that you can see your fingernails (not the other way!) gives a stronger one. Anything stronger is achieved with the help of your seat and back muscles, not by stiffening your wrist, tensing your arms and pulling. The latter is the beginner's common error and results in resistance or deadening of the horse's response, leaning on the bit and going heavily on the forehand.

Finally, remember that your hands do not work alone, but in conjunction with your elbows and shoulders, back and thence the rest of your body. The rein aid, the weight aid and the leg aid must all occur separately but appropriately co-ordinated for the horse to understand them.

It is completely impossible for the rider to think consciously and simultaneously of doing several different things at once and this is why so many lessons end in red-faced frustration. If you follow the principles outlined above and teach your body progressively to feel its way to effective riding, building up the right feel one step at a time, you will find that you make progress with much greater satisfaction and much less physical effort.

Herr Arthur Kottas, chief rider of the Spanish Riding School of Vienna and renowned both for his riding and his teaching, once said that a riding session should not leave you feeling exhausted, but as though you have just had a really good massage – in other words, warm, comfortable and relaxed.

In conclusion, while we hope this chapter has given you some new ideas and ways of overcoming riding problems, it is no substitute for being out there with your horse trying the ideas out and improving your mutual efforts at communication. There is also no substitute for good, understanding instruction. Shop around, until you find a sympathetic instructor who speaks your language. The books on equitation noted in the 'Further Reading' list will also expand upon the ideas outlined here and give you more ways to establish your riding with understanding of the horse.

Chapter 7

Riding Out

You've been practising your position and body alignment and are developing that all-important feel. Perhaps you have had a couple of lessons, or have persuaded a friend to help you school at home. Now, it is a warm Saturday morning and the perfect time to go for a long ride. The spring grass is starting to come through and as your horse steps out eagerly, you are aware that it is feeling fresh. However, you remember to soften your focus and breathe all the way down to the bottom of your lungs. You run a quick check list to see if you are tense anywhere and you keep a light, even contact on the reins.

When you start any work with your horse it is wise to spend a few minutes warming up in walk in order to let the horse stretch its muscles and prepare for more strenuous exercise. Allow the horse to carry its head long and low and do not expect it to come 'on the bit' straight away. Keep it moving actively and establish the four-beat rhythm without hustling it out of its natural stride. In this way, you encourage the horse to keep its attention on you and not on everything else in the vicinity. Once the horse is settled and moving well, you can shorten your reins slightly and, with a 'squeezing the sponge' action on the inside rein, coupled with soft leg aids, ask for a little more engagement.

This is where you begin to understand what the mechanics of riding feel like. If your seat is balanced and soft, allowing the horse's back to rise and fall under you, with your hips free and open, the horse can respond to your aids by bringing its hind legs further underneath itself, rounding its back more and, ultimately, raising its forehand. The result of these developments is called 'self carriage'. A trained horse should be able to achieve this if the rider merely sits and rides correctly. An untrained horse needs to be ridden correctly and given time – months or even years, depending upon the level of training aspired to – for its musculo-skeletal system to develop the necessary strength and suppleness. In the meantime, the rider must make allowances, such as riding with a lighter seat when appropriate and avoiding asking too much intensity of work, or too many different things too quickly in succession.

If you ride incorrectly, the musculo-skeletal system will also develop incorrectly and the horse will not build up the right kind of strength and suppleness to carry a rider well. Instead, there will be undesirable muscle development in some areas and muscle wastage in others, accompanied by excessive and abnormal strain on joints, tendons and ligaments, with a commensurately increased risk of injury. All this will limit the horse's ability to perform as a riding horse, let alone as a competition horse.

An appreciation of the mechanics of riding and making the effort to ride well is intrinsic to caring for your horse properly and as vital as giving attention to its feed, accommodation, health, etc. As any equine vet knows, many apparently physical problems can be traced back to unbalanced riding or misguided training.

As you ride along, do not let your attention focus on your hands. It is very easy, when you first attempt to get that feeling of lightness in the hand and impulsion from behind, to let your hands take over, stiffen your wrists and arms and pull in the effort to get the horse to flex and come 'on the bit'. The horse might also try to gull you by leaning on the bit, or snatching at the reins and pulling you forwards, out of balance. Do not let it succeed. Keep your feel on the reins light, with your ribcage raised and concentrate on the feeling from behind and underneath you and the sequence of steps.

Horses, especially those that have not been well schooled, are adept at avoiding working correctly.

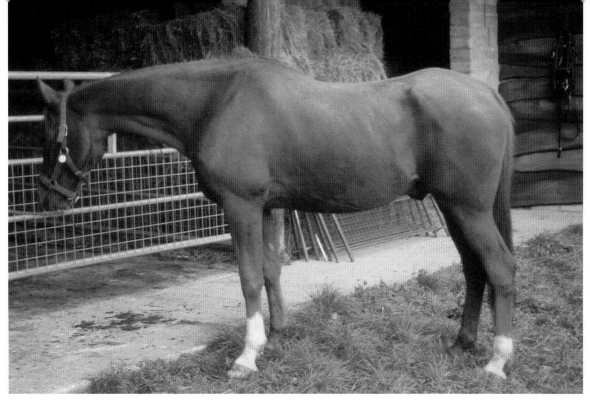

This horse is lacking in muscle development along its topline. There are hollows in front of the shoulders, behind the withers, along the spine and to either side of the tail. This is due partly to under-nourishment but also to incorrect riding over a period of years.

This angle shows more clearly the sunken appearance of the back.

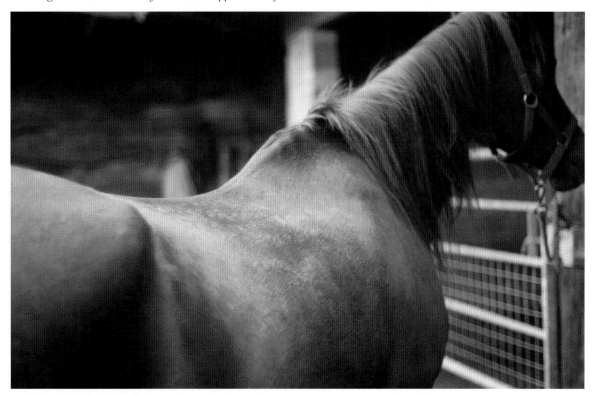

So, if the horse does not want to do it, why should you insist? The answer lies in the fact that nature did not design horses for us to ride. They might seem ideally suited for the purpose, since they have a shoulder that keeps the saddle in place and a pad of muscle along the back for us to sit on, plus a rib cage shaped perfectly for our legs to mould around. However, nature designed the horse to carry the bulk of its bodyweight slung underneath its spine, not perched on top. If we want the horse to carry our weight, as well as its own, we must encourage its body to adapt so that it can do so with the minimum of effort, energy expenditure and risk of damage. It is the training process that is hard work for the horse. As correct training develops, the horse can carry the rider with increasing ease. Without correct training, the horse compensates for the rider's weight in the easiest way it can, but in doing so puts too much strain on its musculo-skeletal system. Taking the line of least resistance causes more damage in the long term. One of the joys of training young horses is to watch their gradual realisation that it is easier to do what you ask than to evade you.

As you ride your horse forwards, the necessity of the independent seat should become increasingly clear. Wherever you want your horse to go, it must have the freedom to go there. If you sit with your weight shifted over to one side and a collapsed hip, or if you are perched over its shoulders, or slumped down on the back of the saddle, you are restricting that freedom, not just a little, but to the extent that your aids are incomprehensible to the horse and it cannot make the desired response, while its body is seriously inconvenienced by your unbalanced weight. To punish it for disobedience in such circumstances, whether by more forceful means, or merely by kicking with your legs and pulling on the reins, shows a serious lack of understanding and a complete loss of the ability to communicate. Sadly, this scenario is all too common and often involves people who truly want to understand their horse and do their best for it.

This horse, Kelly, is on the forehand, taking all of the weight through her shoulders and front legs. Her 'rump high' conformation and straight shoulder make it more difficult for her to balance herself.

ABOVE: *In this photo, going slightly uphill, she presents a better picture though in both photos the rider is 'perched'.*

Let us assume that you are not such a person, but have discovered the joy of sitting in balance and harmony with your horse. If you were at all nervous of riding to begin with, you will discover that in pursuing the goal of an independent seat, another remarkable thing happens. The ability to ride in balance gives you considerably greater security in the saddle and, since you feel safer and in much less danger of falling off, your confidence will increase. As your confidence increases, you will find it easier to focus on the right 'feel' for the aids

LEFT: *This horse, although only four years old, has excellent riding conformation. He has a pleasing arch to his neck, which is well set on to a long, sloping shoulder. Good withers keep the saddle in place on a short, strong back, which flows into long, strong hind quarters. He has adequate bone and straight, rhythmic action.*

at the right time and in the right place.

When you ride in the arena, the surroundings are static and it is relatively easy to gain the horse's attention and keep it on the job. When you ride out, the scenery is constantly changing and horses like to enjoy the view as much as anyone. In fact, the changing view is of more importance to the horse's mentality than it is to yours. As a creature of flight, rather than 'fight', it is essential for the horse to spot danger from a distance and to know which way it can escape. On the other hand, when you are riding, you want your horse to accept you as its leader, to trust you and to keep its attention on you.

The younger and more novice the horse, the more important it is to let it stop and look closely at potential new dangers and to look around generally and take in its surroundings. As your partnership with the horse develops, it should be more willing to accept your judgement, quicker to accept new experiences and be less mesmerised by every new and distant horizon. Find a happy medium when out hacking. Do not give in to every whim and when you decide its time to concentrate on work, then that is what you do. However, at other times, give your horse a chance to relax and enjoy the countryside, let it stand and absorb the view while having a breather and filling up on air. Horses, with their sharp eyesight, often show us things we would

have missed. Trot up a hill on the bit to improve fitness, but hack down the other side on a long rein.

Hacking should never be boring. There is always something new to teach your horse, or something you can learn. Many of the things you practise in the arena can also be practised out hacking. Transitions, for example, can be improved as easily along a track as in the school. It is surprising how many people forget all about their flatwork as soon as they go for a ride, allowing their horses to run on, on the forehand, falling into trot or canter and shuffling back down through the gaits. Yet riding is a much more pleasant experience if you just remember to keep your horse balanced and give clear aids for changes of gait. It should become an automatic action that you do almost without thinking about it.

Lateral work improves your horse's concentration as well as its suppleness. Leg yielding from one side of a path to the other is easy to practise and shoulder in is very useful for improving obedience and passing 'bogeys'. The turn on the forehand comes in handy when you are opening and closing gates from horseback and if you take the time to practise, your horse will become very adept at helping you.

Natural terrain can also add interest and variety for you and your horse. On rough ground, you need to pick your way carefully to avoid risking injury to

Enjoying an autumn hack, Tara has spotted something interesting and has paused to look.

The turn about the forehand is a useful exercise . . . like all exercises it should be performed in balance and with rhythm.

your horse's feet and legs. On better going you can enjoy a canter. At all gaits, try to maintain rhythm and a controlled speed so that you build up your horse's fitness and strength with the minimum risk of strain. Even at a gallop, your horse should be under control and you should be able to stop when you wish. A slow canter is more energy efficient than a flat out trot and if you can teach your horse to canter rhythmically, in hand, this is a very comfortable way to ride. Do not get into the habit of going flat out on every stretch of green and then having to stop while your horse gasps for breath for ten minutes at the end.

Hills are good for improving your horse's strength and fitness, but how do you ride up and down in a balanced way? Possibly you will have been told to lean forwards and perhaps stand in the stirrups to get the weight off the horse's back going up and to lean back going down. In fact, the best place for your weight to be is in the horse's centre of balance, as always. Going uphill, the horse should push itself up by bringing its hind legs well under its body and using the power of its hind

quarters. The best place for you to be is sitting centrally in the saddle, with your lower body at an angle of 90° to the slope and your upper body at 90° to the horizontal plane. In this way you can keep your legs on the horse and avoid them swinging back and kicking it in the stifles. The horse's shoulders remain free to take advantage of the momentum from the rear end.

Similarly, going down, your lower body remains at 90° to the slope and your upper body at 90° to the horizontal. This may feel like leaning back, but in fact is upright. If anything, if the horse is moving at speed down the hill, your upper body should be inclined very slightly forwards. Your weight should drop evenly down your legs on either side of the horse and if your leg joints are free from tension, your heels will drop down and you will be balanced and stable in the saddle. Going downhill, as well as uphill, the horse needs to bring its hocks as far under its body as possible. If it tries to go downhill with its weight on the forehand, it will be unable to balance itself and will increase speed until it is plunging down at a fast trot, with the rider out of

An easy hand canter is an economical pace.

control on top. It will also be in danger of tripping and falling. However, with its quarters engaged, the horse can maintain a rounded outline and negotiate a slope without putting excessive strain on its front legs. Good hill riding needs to be practised on progressively steeper terrain.

The countryside is full of 'bogeys', from yapping dogs to lorries with air brakes, from washing lines to the bird that flies out of the hedge under your nose. Most accidents – barring the dangerous and irresponsible driver – result from inattention and lack of preparation on the part of the rider. A horse on a loose rein is not really under your control and if you are riding like a passenger, instead of the driver, you will be that much slower to react in the event of trouble. The bird in the hedge is the simplest example. If you have been slopping along on a loose rein and your horse suddenly leaps ten feet sideways, what are your chances of staying in the saddle? If, on the other hand, you have been riding in balance, with just a little attention on your horse, you will be prepared and although you might get a bit of a shock, you are unlikely to be unseated. Your body will react to the situation before you have time to think about it and will follow the horse's movement. If you are really prepared, a squeeze on the rein and a leg against the horse's side might prevent it from shying altogether.

The most dangerous hazard for the rider today is traffic and all horses need to be acclimatised to it in

Going uphill, the horse must bring its hind legs well underneath its body. The rider stays in the saddle with legs at the girth.

a progressive and non-threatening way, which is sometimes easier said than done. The amount of traffic your horses see will depend upon where you live. We are lucky to be in a rural area, where tractors are more of a hazard than buses and we do

Downhill, the horse still needs to bring the hind legs under the body. The rider sits quietly upright, with the seat in the saddle and the legs at the girth.

On this slope the horse has become distracted and fallen on her forehand.

not ride on main roads. We still take the time to accustom our youngsters to traffic gradually. Their earliest experience is of a truck driving around their fields and when they finally venture out, it is in company with an experienced horse and with the rider wearing a 'Caution – Young Horse' vest, or more effective still, an 'L' plate.

Learning to cross water is another experience which many horses find daunting, but fortunately the lesson usually only has to be learned once. A lead from an experienced horse will often have the desired effect, but some horses still resist and need more encouragement. The answer is to be patient and persistent. The horse must be ridden forwards, that is, you must maintain contact with the bit and keep your legs on firmly, ensuring that the horse faces the direction which it is required to go. Some people give away the contact in the belief that the horse will go forwards better if its head is free. This is rarely the case and merely results in the horse turning away from the problem, while maintaining contact gives the horse confidence that you, its

leader, are still there. Equally futile and negative are flapping the reins and kicking with your heels, either of which will just irritate the horse and give it an excuse to back or turn away.

It is popularly held that once you start to tackle a problem, such as going through water, you must not stop until you succeed, or you will never win the battle. This is probably not true, although if you do give up the first time, for example, if you are on your own and you go back next time with a friend to give you a lead, it may take longer to get past the horse's initial reluctance to approach the stream. However, it is preferable not to start schooling your horse for such a problem unless you can set the whole thing up in advance, that is, take the friend with you and know that you have enough time to see the lesson through.

All other hazards should be approached in the same way. In other words, give the horse a chance to have a look and discover that the hazard is not that dangerous. Often this is enough for the horse to accept the situation and carry on calmly. If it does balk, just be quietly persistent. Keep your leg on

101

Rough terrain on a frosty morning. The horse must stay balanced and focused, while the rider looks ahead to where she is going.

and a steady contact and, nine times out of ten, the horse will accept your insistence fairly quickly. If it takes longer, then it takes longer, but do not become impatient and try to force the horse past by shouting, kicking, or using your whip repeatedly. If you do this you just antagonise the horse when it is already unsettled and set the scenario for another battle next time, whereas quiet persistence tells the horse there is really nothing to worry about and although it may continue to hesitate until its confidence grows, it will progressively accept the different things you meet out riding.

The extent to which you encounter difficulties with your developing partnership with your horse depends to a considerable degree on your attitude to new experiences. Remember that while you might be struggling to understand your horse's body language, it already has a masters degree in understanding yours. If, when you encounter an obstacle, your body language says 'Oh dear, this is a worrying thing. I'm afraid of it or what might happen,' the horse will hear you loud and clear and will not go anywhere near the frightening monster. On the other hand, if your body language says 'Oh, look, this is interesting, lets go and take a closer look,' your horse might take a little convincing, but it will not be afraid and it *will* do as you ask.

This does not mean you have to be foolhardy. It just means that if you are riding a horse and you have an obstacle to deal with, whether it is a gate to open, a tractor to pass, or a ditch to jump, it is essential to maintain your effective, tension-free riding position and avoid the automatic tensing of your body that comes with worry or nervousness. The more you practise inhibiting the unhelpful responses of fear and the more accustomed you become to balanced riding, the easier it will be. Do not try to tell yourself not to be afraid – that does not work. What you do is refuse to let your body make the habitual physical response that fear initiates. When fear tells you, 'Get ready to jump!', tell your body, 'Do not get ready to jump!' and consciously prevent all those fear/tension responses from blocking your ability to control what you do.

Chapter 8

Shows and Competitions

If your aim is to take your horse to shows and competitions, you need to be confident that it will behave appropriately in public. Inadequate preparation for this big step can result in trauma for the inexperienced owner. The horse is simply overwhelmed by all the new sights and sounds and becomes distracted and excitable.

The solution is to prepare as much as possible beforehand. Ideally, young horses are introduced to a variety of public experiences before being sold as riding horses. In reality this may not be the case. If you have acquired an older horse, it may be happy about some things and less happy about others, depending upon the education it received and the events of its earlier life.

Behaviour in company

The most important thing to ascertain is your horse's behaviour in the company of others. If it is kept on a yard, with others coming and going, you will have a pretty good idea of its attitude towards strangers. If it is kept alone, or with one or two constant companions, you will have to find out.

The way any individual horse interacts with others is a very important part of its life. It is essential to understand your own horse's attitudes and to be aware that it will not react to every other horse in the same way. Remember that left to their own devices, horses quickly establish a pecking order. Under saddle, the rider's wishes must be paramount, but the basic instinct is still there.

The start of a race – a time when you need your horse to be listening to you and under control!

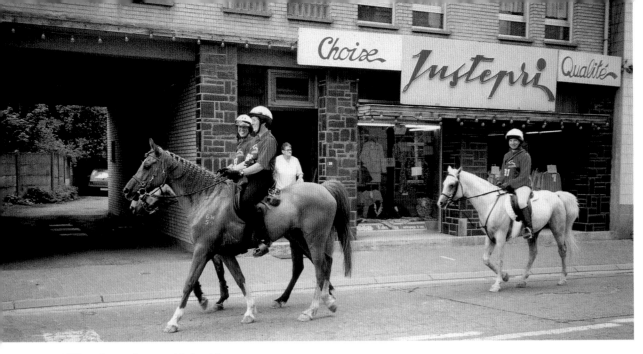

Riding first or last, or side by side.

A horse that is well schooled for riding is expected virtually to ignore other horses while being ridden and most will comply with this expectation, most of the time. However, situations occur that can upset even the best-behaved horse and you should make it second nature to be aware all the time of the safety of your horse's position in relation to other horses. All too often, at shows and events, horses are seen being led or ridden close behind others. If you do this and you or your horse get kicked, it is your fault. Even though horses are more or less trained to accept others in close proximity, if one is startled, or feels pressurised, its natural response will reassert itself. It can be reprimanded and its training can be reinforced, but

in the meantime, someone may have a broken leg, so do not put yourself or your horse into a position where you might be on the receiving end.

Horses are selective in how they behave towards others. We have one which has never threatened a stranger when out in public, but kicked out at its regular companion when it came close alongside on a narrow path. The rider was not expecting the incident and was unprepared to prevent it, while the horse took the opportunity to reassert its habitual dominance over the other.

A horse which does lash out at another, for whatever reason, should be reprimanded strongly and instantaneously. If you are more than a split second late, the retribution will not have the desired

Horses at a multi-day endurance ride, turned out in electric fenced corrals, all quite happy and relaxed.

effect, which is to deter the horse from kicking next time it gets the idea. At the same time you must make sure that the horse's quarters are turned immediately away from the other horse, so that if it strikes out again there is no danger of contact. If you feel your horse tense itself to kick, use a strong leg aid quickly to turn its quarters out of the way in conjunction with a growling, threatening voice and as soon as you are in a safe position, ride strongly forwards.

If you ride out in company, which is one way to prepare your horse for meeting others at shows, you will find that it goes better with one horse than with another. In certain company, your horse may be subservient and in other company, dominant.

Although the horse has its own rules for relating to other horses, it must learn that in company or not, it must give its primary attention to you as its leader. This occurs as a natural progression of handling and riding. The more you interact with your horse, on and off its back, the better established its responses to you will become.

When you ride out in company, especially if it is always with the same people, it becomes easy to fall into the habit of a particular horse always going first or last, or acting as the lead horse, while others follow. Then, if you try to change the order of progression, or put another horse in front, the horses nap and get irritable. Therefore, make a point of changing around frequently during a ride. The horse that always wants its nose in front and pulls or plays up if it is behind is not listening to you; nor is the horse that is always content to slug along with its nose on another's tail. See Chapter 12 for coping with the problem of napping.

Well-schooled horses, when riding out, should go happily in front or behind, or alongside one another. They should wait for one another when required, go away from one another when required and respond to the rider's aids regarding gait, speed and pace, rather than just doing what the other horse does. As herd animals, horses are great copycats and easily fall into the pony trekking syndrome of 'We all canter here, trot here and walk here.' Once they develop such a habit, it is very hard to break, so do not encourage it when you ride out with friends. Take turns to go in front, stand and wait while your friend does a bit of schooling in an open space, or jumps the logs on a path and get your friend to wait behind, instead of always giving you a lead, when there is something scary to pass.

Playing ground games with your horse, as

In the heat of the moment it is sometimes difficult to leave enough space, but if you ride too close, the horse in front cannot be blamed for any reaction.

explained in Chapter 4, can be extended to introducing the kind of things you are likely to meet at shows. You can play music while you work, put up flags (your old T-shirts will do, you do not need your national banner) and dream up any number of distractions for your horse to look at. The key to success, however, is to introduce new things progressively. It may surprise you how quickly your horse learns to accept them.

Your first show

When you first take your horse out in public, pick a small, informal event. Even if the horse has done it all before, you are going to be a little nervous if it is your first time, so you do not want a competition that is too demanding. If your horse has not done it all before, it should be able to cope with a small show with an informal atmosphere fairly easily. After a few small shows, the bigger crowd and heightened atmosphere of a larger event will not seem so daunting. Local riding club fixtures are ideal for beginning your competitive career.

Arrive in good time, so that you do not get flustered trying to get ready and allow yourself plenty of time to warm up or work in. Say hello to friends but, before your class, keep your attention on the job. When riding in the practice arena, remember to breathe and use your peripheral vision to stay aware of the position of other horses, so that you avoid embarrassing collisions. Remember your riding technique: things often go to pieces at a show, because the rider is nervous about the competition and becomes tense beforehand.

You have already discovered that nervousness creates tension that blocks effective riding. In addition, your horse can sense your tension and will react with tension itself, alert for the danger which is obviously worrying you! The only way out of this impasse is to prevent your body from reacting to your nervousness. Exactly how you do this may be something it will take time to discover. For some people a particular image may work, others may imagine they are listening to soothing music. If you find the key which unlocks your independent seat (one rider we know imagines herself sitting on two squashed tomatoes!), it is fairly easy to make the connection with the rest of your body.

You may have heard international showjumpers

say that once they are in the ring they do not see or hear the crowd. This is the result of being entirely focused on what they are doing, but it is not some magic trick. You can achieve exactly the same thing by letting your awareness centre on the responses of your body to the horse's movement, stride by stride. To ride well, your attention must be on the riding, moment by moment, not on whether you will make a fool of yourself or even whether your horse will jump the upright which is five fences ahead. Nothing matters except what is happening underneath you right this second. By expanding your conscious awareness of your whole body, you will increase your ability to be 'as one' with your horse. With time, you will find that everything seems to slow down, you will have time to give precise, well-controlled aids, the rest of the world will recede and nothing will exist except your horse, yourself and the movement.

The rider's ability to be relaxed, yet focused, is a very powerful tool. Imagine you arrive at the show and unload your horse. As you remove its travelling gear and tack up, you struggle to control an attack of 'butterflies'. You feel cold, your muscles twitch with tension and your hands tremble as you fasten buckles. Your horse senses your disquiet and becomes fidgety. You get cross because it will not stand still. Eventually you mount and, because you are keyed up, your seat and legs tense up and start to grip, while your hands tighten on the reins. The horse becomes irritated and mirrors your nervousness. It starts to take short, quick steps, swishes its tail, tosses its head and maybe even threatens other passing horses. As you try to warm up, your horse is distracted and will not listen to you, its head is up and its neck is as stiff as an iron bar. How can you hope for a successful performance?

Now imagine a different scenario. You arrive at the show and unload. The 'butterflies' threaten, but you invoke whatever image helps you inhibit your habitual reaction – perhaps you imagine all the butterflies settling down to roost. You consciously free your body of tensions and maybe do some stretching exercises to warm yourself up before you mount. While you tack up, you think about your breathing and let the air flow in all the way to the bottom of your chest. This in itself has a calming effect. Your calmness reassures your horse and so it remains tractable. When you mount, you take a few moments to sort yourself out, soften your back and

Introducing new things progressively: Elf is introduced to long reins. First, Becky shows her the lunge line.

Becky walks around Elf, gradually accustoming her to the feel of the line over her body. In previous lessons Elf has learned to stand still on command.

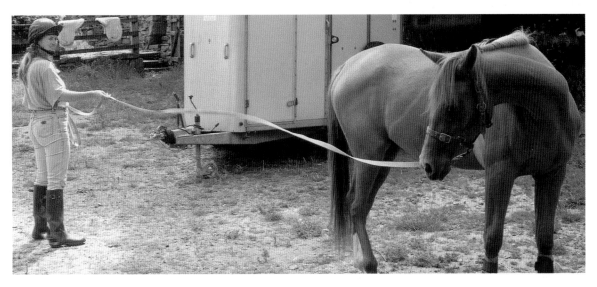

Eventually Becky can move away from Elf's body and wiggle the line at her, without her moving off. Elf is just curious and turns her head to look.

seat and check your position. As you ride forwards, you continue to breathe and monitor your position by checking on how each part of your body feels. With your direction focused upon your riding in this way, you do not have time to worry about being nervous, while your horse, in the absence of any signs of tension from you, moves forwards calmly and confidently in a relaxed frame and paying attention to your aids.

You might think this is easier said than done and, obviously, things do not change overnight. However, as you work at your riding and improve your techniques and confidence, overcoming nervousness also becomes easier as you find there is less to be nervous about!

Mental rehearsal is one method that may be helpful. It is based on the idea that if we think negative thoughts they will become established and,

Before getting down to serious work, or a competition, working in should help you and your horse to relax and become focused on the task in hand.

conversely, if we think positive thoughts, they will be effective. Most of us, after a competition, may tend to dwell on the negative side, even if we do reasonably well. For example, we mentally re-ride the one movement in the dressage test that we got wrong. By going over it again and again, we establish it in our consciousness so that next time, we will probably do exactly the same wrong thing again. Mental rehearsal, however, is a way of practising the positive aspects of your riding when dismounted. What you do is to imagine yourself riding a good test or round, as you would like to ride it, in the smallest detail possible. Ideally, imagine the feel of each stride of the competition from start to finish. The more precisely you can do this, the easier the actual test or round will be. The theory is that your body will recall the correct feeling and will do that, instead of the wrong thing.

When working in, keep your attention on yourself and on your horse. As far as possible, ignore what everyone else is doing, apart from keeping an awareness of your horse's personal space and safety. Begin by loosening up and encouraging your horse to relax, working long and low to stretch its neck and back. The amount of work you need to do will depend on your individual horse's temperament and stage of training. Initially, until you learn through experience the best approach, it is better to do too little than too much

and to keep the horse calm and settled rather than getting it over enthusiastic. A slightly lack-lustre performance can be worked on and improved, but if everything has got out of control and gone to pieces there is nothing for it but to rebuild your work from the beginning.

In-hand shows

If you are showing in hand, much the same principles apply. Thorough preparation at home and attention to detail will pay dividends in the ring. Groundwork games, time taken to teach the horse to keep its attention on you, despite the distractions of the ring, to stand up correctly for the judge and to trot out well, the introduction of music, flags, etc. are all essential aspects of the education of the in-hand horse. Holding a mock show with a few friends can be a valuable experience for the novice horse and will tell you how well you have done your training before you get to the actual show.

What you do when you arrive, such as taking the horse for a walk to let it look at the showground, or keeping it quietly by the box, will depend upon its temperament and experience. Likewise, the amount of working in needed, such as lungeing, is something you will learn through experience.

The nervousness of a handler on the ground can affect the horse's behaviour just as much as that of someone on its back, so the same principles for

ABOVE: *A master showman presenting a winning Arab mare at an international show. He is totally focused on his task, while keeping out of the horse's way and timing his run to her trot, to show her to the best advantage.*

overcoming it apply. Mentally rehearse the perfect trot out, breathe deeply and slowly and let your body language communicate the right messages to your horse.

Keeping the competition in perspective

Individual horses react differently to going to shows and competitions. Some cannot wait to get into the lorry or trailer and enjoy the whole experience. Some become stressed, worried or nervous for a variety of reasons, while others show similar behaviour but in excitement or anticipation. Still others just accept the whole business with equanimity, as just another daft thing the humans want them to do.

RIGHT: *This young Thoroughbred was wide eyed with the excitement of his first show, but a sound and secure upbringing resulted in his first rosette.*

Riders too have different attitudes. If you build up all your hopes and expectations to success, failure can bring crushing disappointment. It is far better to look on any competition as just another step in the overall training and career of your horse. If you treat each competition as a training exercise, you will keep a sensible perspective and be able to build on whatever the result may be. After all, the horse does not particularly care about winning cups and rosettes, although it may well enjoy being made a fuss of when it does well.

Planning a competition programme

Horses may not care about trophies, but they do sense the atmosphere of excitement and anticipation that accompanies a competition morning and they may react in various ways. We had one mare which, when she first came to our yard, would drip with sweat within a few minutes of anyone walking into her stable with her travelling gear. This mare caused us many headaches. She was easy to handle, very kind, no trouble to load or travel, loved her work and was very competitive. However, she was extremely sensitive to her environment. Being prepared to travel was her cue to develop acute diarrhoea and I have seen her stand and shake with nervous excitement. On trips away, her stable had to be to her liking, or she might box walk all night. She was a strong, enthusiastic ride and in endurance competition she would run on pure adrenaline beyond the point of physical exhaustion if we had let her. She was a talented, but very complex personality and it took us three seasons to discover how to compete her effectively, keeping weight on her and her stress levels in check. Now, as a brood mare in her late teens, she is still the boss of her

A horse that was not fit enough on a drip at the end of an endurance event. Treatment was given immediately and the horse has perked up and is well on the way to recovery.

At the end of every training exercise, check your horse's legs for heat or other signs of injury.

field and behaves with the same keyed up determination she exhibited when competing.

Stress can have other odd effects. The same mare, when working, had a large unsightly sarcoid. When she retired, it gradually diminished and, finally, disappeared.

Competition work should be pleasurable for the horse, so it is important to monitor its attitude and progress and to ensure that its prior training is appropriate for the task in hand. The type of training you do will obviously depend upon the discipline in which you compete, but you need to be aware of the dangers of both over and under training. Signs of over training include loss of condition, muscle atrophy and stiffness, lameness problems, loss of appetite, poor coat condition and a mental attitude that changes from equable or enthusiastic to sour and unwilling. If you do not train enough, the horse will either not understand what is expected of it, or not be fit enough to perform successfully. The horse which labours its way home, falls, or injures itself on the cross-country course is typical of this.

Once you begin competing, enthusiasm may get the better of discretion and competitors who drag their horses to every available event, every weekend throughout the year, are a familiar sight. Before long, the horses become disillusioned and fed up with the whole business, as well as suffering the effects of repeated physical stress, which may manifest itself in many small ways, without sufficient time between events to recover fully. A horse that is in continual low-grade pain, from sore back muscles, minor strains, bruises, stiffness or just generally tired and stressed, is a miserable companion. Such horses often appear dull and disinterested in their surroundings. When the physical problems really begin to bother them, they

111

start to refuse fences, nap or otherwise perform badly. The type of owner who allows a situation to get to this stage, through being inconsiderate, or merely unobservant, is then likely to begin to punish the horse for disobedience.

To have a successful competition season, you need to plan ahead and to prepare your horse appropriately. Aim to build up your training to peak for a particular event, then allow a sufficient wind down and recovery period before gradually building up again. The recovery period is as important as the training sessions. It allows bones, tendons and ligaments to strengthen and the damage to muscle cells, which is an inevitable response to training, to repair. Do not be caught up in the 'every weekend' syndrome. Instead, do something different with your horse on the intervening weekends – go on a training course, or go for a picnic, or commune with your horse while you pick blackberries, mend the fence or clean out the ditch in its field. In this way you will keep its interest in life as well as keeping it in good physical health.

Keep a close eye on your horse's condition. Competition stress can easily cause a horse to lose weight. If it goes off its food, starts to lose muscle (as opposed to just getting rid of excess fat), or exhibits any other signs of strain, such as loss of enthusiasm or other changes of character, step back and ask yourself why. If you cannot find out why, consult someone who can – such as your vet, trainer or physiotherapist – before you go to any more competitions. Back off and take the time to put matters right. If you respond to signs of trouble quickly, they will probably be easy to correct. If you continue competing without sorting out an imminent problem, it could lead to months, or perhaps years of heartache.

Ideally the scope of any competition you tackle should extend your horse's experience, but be well within its current level of capability. Experienced competition riders aim to train to a level that is slightly higher than the one at which they compete. For example, a dressage horse competing at novice level will be learning elementary movements at home. A horse trials rider will take the opportunities offered to school round a cross-country course the day following an event, or will hire a course where they can practise over various types of fences, so

that the horse is not expected to tackle a new type of obstacle cold at a competition.

Whatever your discipline, over-facing your horse in competition is counter-productive. If the fences are too big, you cannot put them down and re-school your horse from the basics in the middle of a showjumping round. If your horse refuses, or makes a serious blunder, it will go out of the ring with the mistake imprinted in its mind and re-schooling afterwards will be more difficult.

Asking your horse to do too much, whether in frequency or intensity, will eventually result in a horse which is fed up with the whole business and unwilling to do what is asked. Putting such unnecessary problems right is the bread and butter of many 'expert' trainers. In all your competition efforts remember that horses learn by repetition and association, in logical progressive steps, while their physical ability to perform depends upon a sensible training programme in conjunction with appropriate management of health, feeding and condition.

The right horse in the wrong career

Sometimes it is necessary to accept that the horse you have got is either simply not suited to the discipline in which you are interested, or is not capable of competing at the level you desire. Your cob may go all day, but will not win any races. Occasionally, the horse's temperament or attitude is unsuitable, often because of what the horse has done in a former career. Some Thoroughbreds that have raced, for instance, never settle to work in the show ring, although others, with patient, understanding training, succeed spectacularly.

If you genuinely have a round peg in a square hole, the only answer is to change your discipline or change your horse. However, there are many other reasons for horses failing to achieve their owners' desires. The wrong feeding, the wrong training, lack of communication between horse and trainer, lack of observation of the horse by the trainer and too much being asked of a horse that is too young or too inexperienced are just a few of these. If you want to succeed in competition, you must be observant and listen to what your horse is telling you, then act upon what you see.

Chapter 9

The Mare and Foal

The mare: understanding the female psyche

When we are breeding horses to be sold on, we hope for colts, which can be castrated and sold as geldings. The market for geldings is always stronger than that for fillies, due to the common belief that they are easier to manage and do not have 'hormonal problems'. However, when we are breeding horses to keep for ourselves to ride, we hope for fillies. Given the choice, we prefer to ride mares.

Why do we suffer from this apparent perversity? Well, everyone has personal preferences and without a shred of scientific evidence to back us up, it is our experience that mares are more fun, more interested in what is going on around them, smarter, more determined and generally braver than geldings. Geldings, on the other hand, are more reliable, equally bold, less inclined to argue with you and do not suffer from cyclical changes of mood. If you want a horse that is going to behave more or less the same every day and not come in season on the morning of a big competition, pick a gelding. But if you want a relationship that is an evolving and fascinating challenge, choose a mare.

In Chapter 1 we looked at various reasons why horses live in herds. However, the over-riding reason is to ensure the reproduction of their genes. For animals that have to roam to find food, the herd provides a stable environment for reproduction. In non-travelling species, territory is the factor that decides who mates with whom. While the stallion's job is to keep the group together, the role of the mare is to lead the way, find water and grazing and to watch for danger. Maybe this is why the mare's temperament is less predictable, and why she is more alert and often sharper to react than the gelding.

A mare's place in the social hierarchy can tell a great deal about her character. Although age often

Rafiki is just a few hours old, but already is trying to discover what his mother finds so interesting about grass.

113

Ria's first foal is on the way.

Tony has cleared the membrane from the foal's nose and renders some gentle veterinary assistance.

A final push from Ria and her new baby emerges into the world.

As Ria recovers, the foal's movements attract her attention. She looks intrigued and slightly surprised, while Tony reassures her.

Rosy and Rafiki have taken a keen interest in the whole process. Ria warns Rafiki to keep his distance as Mimi makes her first attempt to stand.

Ria explores her new baby, continuing the bonding process.

Mimi has the right idea but hasn't quite found what she is looking for.

determines superiority among younger siblings, it is not necessarily the deciding factor among unrelated females. Some mares are just more willing to risk an argument than others, perhaps because they have never had the experience of losing one! Others would rather keep the peace.

A 12-year-old brood mare that came to us on loan was introduced to our three fillies, aged 2, 3 and 4. For the first day they were outraged at the intrusion in their field and, as a group, drove her away to the far side. After 48 hours, the 4-year-old, a dominant but calm individual, became curious and spent an entire day getting to know her new companion, sniffing her all over and following her around. Then it was the turn of the 2-year-old; however, the 3-year-old remained aloof.

It would have been easy to assume that the older mare would easily dominate all three of the youngsters, but she remained subservient, particularly to the 3-year-old, who will not tolerate her in 'her' space. She is quite happy to communicate with either of the others on an individual basis, but when any two are together, she keeps her distance. This mare has visited various different studs and had to get along with numerous strangers during her life. Clearly she has learned that discretion is the better part of being able to rub along with your temporary companions.

Introducing strange mares to one another is always a little nerve wracking. When you have two dominant characters the battle for superiority can go on for days and even when it is apparently settled, can flare up at any time.

The mare's temperament and her place in the hierarchy carry over strongly into her relationship with others – the stallion, her foal and other offspring and her human handlers. The higher up the pecking order she moves, the more strongly and frequently she will challenge her superiors and the less tolerant she will be of insubordination from inferiors.

In a stressful situation, extreme behaviour may occur. For example, if a mare and her foal are cornered, the mare's normal protective attitude may develop into aggression against her handlers. This is likely to happen where the mare is inexperienced, with her first foal, or if she has been infrequently handled and has not learned to trust people. If it is necessary to handle either mare or foal, for example, for veterinary treatment, the handler is then in a very difficult situation.

The mare will normally protect her foal in various ways. The simplest is that when approached, she will simply trot away, keeping her body between the perceived threat and her foal. She will drive away any other horses that approach too close for comfort, including her own older offspring, and she will attack any other animal that threatens her foal, for example, a curious pet dog, or a human she does not know and trust.

It is therefore advisable, even when you know a mare well, to approach her and her new-born foal with caution until she has accepted your presence in close proximity to the foal. Be particularly careful when working with the mare and foal in a stable or any confined space. However much she trusts you, any mare will react to any perceived threat to her foal, even if you thought your move was completely innocent. Taking care means making sure the mare knows exactly where you are and what you are doing at all times, avoiding any sudden or unpredictable moves and never putting yourself

between mare and foal. If the foal needs to be caught, for example, for a blood sample to be taken for registration purposes, make sure that the mare is caught also and held where she can see the whole procedure. Maybe you have fed her every day for ten years but she will still knock you down if you are in the way when she is upset and wants to get to her foal.

A mare that is well used to being handled and to the presence of humans in her life will quickly adapt to accepting you as part of her foal's life as well, once she is over the trauma of giving birth and the natural anxiety that the presence of the new-born foal brings. If you happen to be there at the birth, some mares may appreciate your presence and reassurance, in which case they will probably also accept you handling the foal immediately. A maiden mare, in particular, may accept this strange newcomer into her life more readily, if a familiar human is there to reassure her that everything is well. Mares vary in the degree of protectiveness

Rosy's whole expression is one of gentle affection as she administers mild early discipline when the foal attempts to leave her side.

Enough is enough! Rosy is aiming for the dog that was running around my feet when I took this photo.

117

Mimi was introduced to humans and given basic imprint training at birth and a day later is quite unconcerned when Tony visits her in the stable, with Ria close by.

She's off. Note how closely Rafiki remains at her side, no matter how she twists or turns.

that they show to their foals. Some may be very protective of their first foal and less so thereafter, while some first-time mothers may lack strong maternal instincts. Therefore, it is very important at the birth and immediately afterwards to allow the mare and foal some time to bond, so that the mare will at least get to know and accept this stranger that she has produced. A few mares actively reject their foals. In the maiden mare this may arise out of anxiety and ignorance and a ticklish resentment of the foal's attempts to suckle. This situation can be resolved by keeping mare and foal stabled at first and restraining the mare so that the foal can suckle until the mare becomes used to the strange sensation. If holding the mare and talking to her quietly are inadequate means of restraint, a twitch can be used (see Chapter 13). The handlers must take care to avoid being kicked and a watch must be kept to ensure that an antagonistic mare does not actually attack her foal. Such incidents are, thankfully, rare. However, they do occur, in which case the foal must be separated from the mare for its own safety. If all attempts to reconcile the mare to motherhood fail, even when the foal has suckled her a few times, it may be necessary to find a foster mother, or rear the foal by hand.

After the first few days of relative privacy, however, most mares welcome visitors and the opportunity to show off their offspring, which by then are lively, inquisitive creatures, already fast on their feet and amazingly well co-ordinated. Our older mare, who has had six foals, is always happy to bring her new offspring for inspection and you can almost hear her thinking 'Oh good, babysitters!' as she leaves junior to the humans and gets busy grazing.

Behaviour to the stallion and reproductive cycle

The mare's attitude to the stallion is normally sexually driven. Out of heat, she will tolerate him, if she knows him and is accustomed to run with him, as she would any other horse, provided he is sensible and polite enough not to make unwanted advances. A mare and stallion used to running together may become the best of friends.

An out of season mare approached by a strange stallion will normally squeal and may strike out, pointedly telling him to keep his distance, particularly if he makes sexually interested noises at her.

As she comes into heat the mare's attitude becomes more coy, in turn rejecting and leading the stallion on until, eventually, at the appropriate time, mating occurs. As she goes off heat, the mare has no compunction in letting the stallion know, in no uncertain terms.

As her cycle affects her attitude towards the stallion, so it may affect her attitude towards her handlers and her work. Being in season can also adversely affect performance and for important competitions, the mare's season can be delayed by the use of a synthetic progesterone called 'Regumate', which is given in the feed.

Colour and temperament

Everyone has a favourite colour, but the chestnut mare is universally maligned. Red hair is reputed to go with a hot temper, but although we have known some lively chestnut mares, including some that are extremely talented, we have never known one that was excessively temperamental or unmanageable. There may be some foundation for the theory that chestnut horses, as with red-haired humans, have more sensitive skin than those with other colouring and perhaps greater care is needed in grooming, tacking up, etc. However, correctly handled, there is no reason why a chestnut mare should be any more difficult than any other horse.

The foal

We mentioned earlier the need for bonding between mare and foal. This is necessary for several reasons, the most fundamental of which is that if a foal and its mother have to run from a predator in the first few hours of its life, they must be able to find each other again, perhaps in a herd comprising many mares and foals. The foal will spend much of its early life asleep. When it wakes up hungry, it must know how to find the mare that will feed it. Imprinting is a special kind of learning process that enables the foal to recognise things that are important to it. Obviously, its own mother is the most important object, but the foal may also imprint on other things.

This observation led Dr Robert Miller, an American veterinary surgeon, to develop the training of new-born foals by imprinting, that is, by exposing them to experiences and objects that they will encounter later on, with the idea that later training will then be easier (see Further Reading). This 'training' is carried out repetitively in the first few hours of life and involves the trainer handling all parts of the foal's body and picking up its feet. Other aspects that may be introduced include tack, clipper noise, loading, proximity of traffic, music, flapping things, etc. Since the foal is comparatively small and easy to restrain and handle, it is relatively safe and easy for the trainer to carry out this work.

It is debatable to what extent the foal actually imprints on such stimuli, as opposed to the regular method of learning by association, and for what period of time it remains susceptible to imprinting

119

TOP: *Rojo makes preliminary advances in the courtship ritual.*

ABOVE: *A mare ready to mate may still initially reject her suitor.*

RIGHT: *The winking vulva, accompanied by frequent urination, indicates that the mare is receptive*

as a method of learning. Orphan foals certainly imprint on their human 'mother' in the absence of the real one and it is thought that early imprinting may be responsible for the sexual preferences of stallions, for example, for mares of a particular colour, later in life. Other evidence, for example, in the choice of which plants to eat, points to foals learning by imprinting.

According to Dr Miller, imprint training of the foal does not interfere with the process of bonding between mare and foal. However, it must be carried out with care that the mare does not become anxious or upset and she must be allowed to smell and lick the foal during the imprinting process. The aim of imprinting is to desensitise the foal to various stimuli. Therefore each stimulus must be performed repeatedly until the foal ceases to react to it. If you cease the stimulus while the foal still resists it (e.g., shaking its head when you wriggle a finger inside its ear), you achieve the opposite effect of sensitising the foal to the stimulus. In its future life, instead of accepting its ears being handled, the foal will be more resistant than if imprinting had never been attempted. Therefore, if this method of training is to be used, it must be done thoroughly and competently.

The period when a foal is open to imprinting may not be longer than 24 hours after birth. However, this does not mean the foal's training cannot continue by the normal methods of habituation. The attention span of the young foal is short, as can be seen when it suddenly loses interest in its visitors, lies down and falls asleep. Its normal waking attention is naturally given to the immediate concerns of living: eating, drinking and other matters of survival. The trainer must be acutely aware how much or how little energy the foal has left for other matters.

One thing we have observed is that young horses, as they grow up, do differentiate between humans as they do other horses and they relate with the most trust to the human with whom they have had the greatest contact early in life, that is, the person who has handled and fed them from an early age. Getting to know a new person is something which takes time and this continues to apply even when horses are older and, for example, are sold on to a new home.

Whether or not you pursue the idea of imprinting, early handling of the foal is strongly advised. It will set the pattern of its relationship with human beings and will make everything that comes later much easier.

Foals grow in strength and agility with astonishing speed, so the earlier the basic lessons are taught, the less of a physical struggle there will be. Natural wariness of the unknown develops within the first day of life, so bringing the mare and foal into the stable for an hour or two, even if the foal was born outside, will give you a chance to get acquainted. If the mother knows and trusts you, the foal will quickly follow suit.

As explained earlier in this book, restraint of the horse's head, and thus of its ability not only to flee, but also to turn freely and look around, is a psychologically frightening situation for it to overcome. The same applies to the young foal and extends even to the feeling of the foal slip or headcollar on its head.

Once the foal is used to you moving around it and stroking it all over, the best way to restrain it is with one arm around its quarters and the other gently around its chest. If the foal is acquiescent and not too big, the proximity of your body may then be enough for it to stay still while you slide your arm forwards over its back, slip the foal slip over its nose and do it up around its neck. It helps if the foal is positioned with its bottom in a corner. Sometimes, the feeling of the noseband is enough for the foal to lunge forwards to escape. Do not try to hang on to the foal slip. It is better to release the foal and start again, with a helper if necessary, rather than risk injury to the foal and upsetting it and its dam.

If a foal slip is fitted within the first day, it is usually easy to do. The foal will probably shake its head a few times in an attempt to get rid of the irritating thing, but will soon give up and seek solace in another meal. The foal slip is only really useful at the very beginning, when the head is too small to take the smallest-sized headcollar. Nylon foal slips and headcollars are not advisable. A young foal's foot can easily become caught up when it lifts it to scratch behind an ear and leather should break if necessary, whereas nylon will not.

The foal's skin is very sensitive and soft, so be sure that your foal slip is well cleaned and the leather soft. Studs frequently leave leather headcollars on foals when they are turned out. However, we feel this is risky even in the best of

121

conditions with post and rail fencing all round. Most fields have places where a headcollar could become snagged and caught up and a broken neck is a sad reward for eleven months of waiting, so do not take the chance. Leave the foal slip on for ten minutes or so initially and stay within sight of the foal, then remove it. Put it on again later in the day.

On subsequent days, you may have the odd difficulty if the foal decides it is not going to play today, but patience and calmness will be rewarded in the end and soon the foal will regard wearing it as a normal part of life. As well as teaching the foal to wear a slip or headcollar, spend a few minutes once or twice a day getting the foal used to being handled. Foals are born curious, which is a bonus for the human trainer.

Put yourself on the foal's level by crouching down when you first make friends with it, so that having a large, dangerous animal looming above does not worry it. Avoid appearing as a threat by looking down or away from the foal as you crouch and allow it to approach you before you try to reach out and touch it. Be patient and allow the foal to sniff you all over. Enjoy the sensation of its warm breath, tickly whiskers and fumbling lips as it tries to make out exactly what you are.

With a shy foal that has not been handled at birth, you may need to do this several times before it will allow you to stroke its shoulder. Do not worry – you have plenty of time before it needs its first vaccinations and foot trimming at three months old.

A bolder foal may accept being handled more rapidly and be just as keen to 'handle' you. It may not be long before you have to begin teaching good manners. This type of foal is also often less willing to accept new experiences and more likely to challenge your authority.

The key to educating a foal is to follow its mother's example. She will not tolerate bad behaviour, biting, or excessive boisterousness and

Early training of the young foal continues in the days after birth. Rafiki is mouthing or 'snapping' at Becky to show his subservience, just as he would to an older horse.

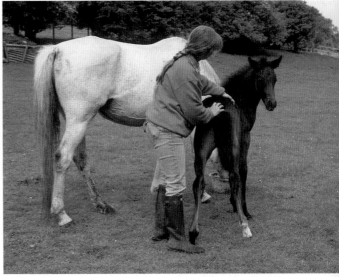

Becky continues the imprint training carried out in the first few hours of Rafiki's life. He is already happy to stand while she runs her hands over him, but his ears and eyes show that his attention is focused on what she is doing.

It's great to have someone scratch the bits you can't reach yourself!

neither should you. It is well worth spending time observing mares and foals together to see how they interact. The easiest way to communicate with a foal is to use a human version of the mare's own body language. When the foal's behaviour is acceptable – when it is feeding, sleeping, exploring without wandering too far away – the mare is calm and has a relaxed body posture. When the foal is naughty – trying to feed when the mare has had enough of it, or boisterously attempting to get her to play with it by biting, striking out or rearing up at her, her body posture changes. She tenses up, turns to face the foal and at the same time makes a threatening gesture with her head and neck, snaking it forwards, tossing it and flattening her ears. She seldom has to do more for the foal to back off.

Similarly, if your foal attempts to barge or bite you, or strike out with its forefeet, the immediate response of a threatening gesture from you will nearly always have the desired effect. You square up to the foal, making yourself look big and threatening and you move towards it, not away. This can sometimes be difficult to do, as the natural impulse is to move out of the way of a bite, barge or threatening hooves. However, a foal's feet do not

do a lot of damage, provided you avoid a direct strike to vulnerable areas of your body (you should, of course, be wearing a safety helmet). In any case, most of the time you are in a safer position closer to the foal's body than at arm's length. So inhibit the urge to step back and instead make your threat posture fast and determined. You can reinforce it with a growl, if you like, but while you must be positive, do make the punishment fit the crime and do not go overboard with your reaction.

As with any other training, a good response from the foal, in this case desisting from the bad behaviour, must be immediately rewarded with praise and rubbing its neck or shoulder in reassurance. This will encourage the foal to think that it is safe with you. It is the beginning of the development of the relationship of trust, with you as the leader and the foal as the follower, so never stint on handing out the reward of comfort in your presence for good behaviour.

With older horses, rubbing the face between the eyes reinforces trust. However, the foal's head is small and sensitive and it may take a while before it is comfortable with this, so rubbing its neck and gently scratching the poll behind the ears are good

a. At four months, Rafiki is happy to accept the headcollar.

b. It's a while since he had a lesson and at first he resists the request to walk. The leadrope is slipped through the headcollar so that it can be released easily if need be.

c. A little encouragement from behind starts him moving. Notice how he leans towards Becky for reassurance.

d. Soon, he happily walks away from his mother.

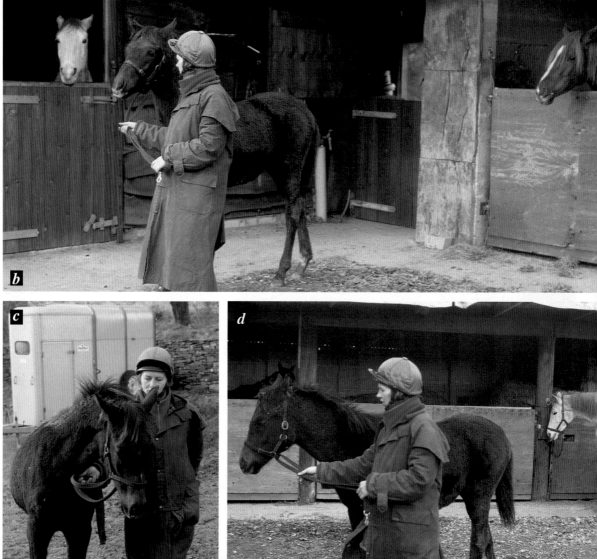

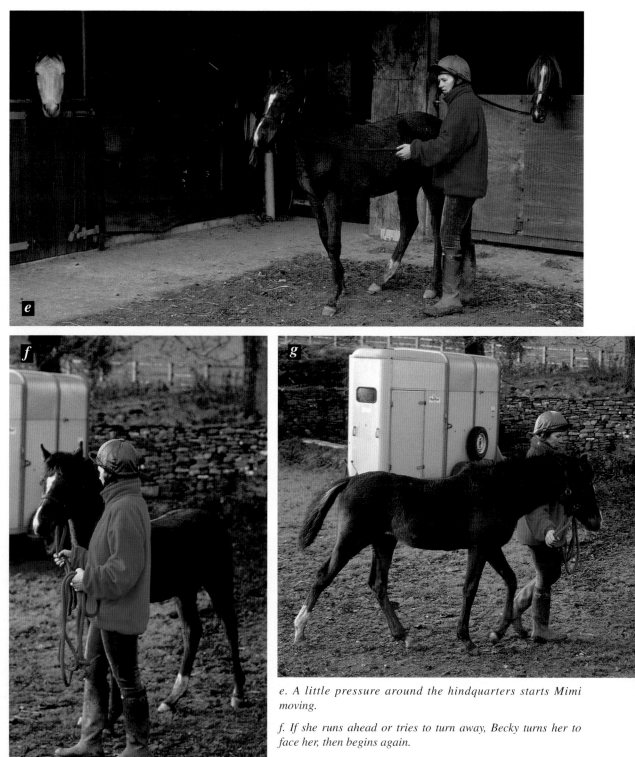

e. A little pressure around the hindquarters starts Mimi moving.

f. If she runs ahead or tries to turn away, Becky turns her to face her, then begins again.

g. Soon Mimi leads happily around the yard.

125

alternatives.

One of the first things a foal needs to learn is how to lead. Having learned to accept wearing headgear, it must learn to accept being controlled by it. As already mentioned, the restraint of its head is a potentially terrifying thing, so the natural response to a human tugging on a leadrope is to tug back, sometimes violently. A frightened foal might shake its head from side to side, go down on its knees, run backwards or rear up and be pulled over in the attempt to break away. The trainer's job is to avoid this battling scenario.

I like to begin in the stable, with one hand on the short lead of the foal slip and the other arm around the foal's quarters. In this non-threatening situation the arm around its quarters can encourage it to step forwards. In two or three sessions, the foal is encouraged to walk around its mother both ways in response to human encouragement.

Leading outside usually has the purpose of taking mare and foal to and from their pasture. To prepare, a long lead is slipped through the ring of the foal slip or under the jaw band of the headcollar and doubled up so that the handler can hold both ends. The leadrope is never clipped to the headgear at this stage. Should the foal pull away, it will be terrified by the 'snake' that is chasing it right under its nose, whereas if the leadrope is simply slipped through and held, the trainer can retain the rope but release the foal if necessary. Some people prefer to begin with a towel held around the foal's neck instead of using the foal slip and leadrope.

The mare is led out and the foal handler takes advantage of the foal's natural inclination to follow. The foal may be worried by the restraint of its head, or things going on outside may distract it. In either case, it may balk. The key to success in teaching a foal to lead is to avoid ever initiating a pull on its head. When it stops, give it a moment to look around, then urge it gently forwards by pressure around the hindquarters. The mare may help by looking back and calling for her foal.

At some point it is inevitable that the foal will put itself in the position of pulling back on the leadrope. A variety of things may then happen. The foal may stop pulling and step forwards as soon as it feels the pressure and thus teach itself to give way. More likely, it will begin to panic and pull back harder, in which case the handler must go with it quickly to take the pressure off so the foal has nothing to pull against. If the foal's reaction is even more violent, and particularly if it rears up, the handler may need to release one end of the leadrope to avoid pulling the foal over and risking injury. The trainer must be

Rafiki enjoys being gently groomed . . .

. . . and decides to join in.

Mimi is quite happy for Becky to pick up her feet.

prepared to move quickly to give the foal the minimum opportunity to fight. Given the possibility that you might need to let the foal escape you, this training obviously needs to be carried out in a safe, enclosed yard or small paddock.

In the first two cases, the moment the foal stops pulling and moves towards the trainer, they must praise and reward it, before encouraging it forwards again from behind. In the last case, the mare should be taken towards the foal, so that it can be quietly caught and the lesson restarted. Usually, the foal that behaves in this way will have frightened itself more than anything else and will think twice before repeating the same performance.

At some point in the procedure, the foal must discover that it is only under pressure when it puts itself under pressure and that moving towards and staying with the trainer relieves that pressure. Thus if the foal pulls on you, the ideal is to let it do so, but without the situation escalating out of control, as in the third scenario above. This will need some quick thinking and manoeuvring on your part. As soon as the foal moves to relieve the pressure, praise and reward it. On the other hand, you must

never be the one to initiate the pulling, as that merely invites the foal to try to get away from you.

Grooming is a natural progression from handling and stroking the foal and most foals quickly learn to enjoy it, although they will want to investigate and sample the taste of your grooming kit, so it is advisable to use old brushes rather than your best new ones. Be gentle in your application of the brush and use a soft one, not a hard-bristled dandy brush. Avoid too much grooming as the foal needs the natural grease in its coat for protection from the weather.

Picking up the feet is easily taught at this age. Get the foal used to your hands running up and down its legs first and when you ask it to pick up a foot, let it put it back down immediately and praise it before repeating with another foot. Gradually, the time you hold the foot up can be increased and eventually you will be able to pick out the hooves. If a foal snatches its legs away, which many do at first, do not insist on picking up the foot, but do not back off either. Continue stroking and rubbing until the foal stands quietly, allowing you to run your hand up and down its cannons and fetlocks. If this is repeated for several days, you can then progress to picking up the foot.

Foals, like the young of any species, need company. Companions can indulge in games, mutual grooming, races, play fights and generally reassure one another and help to build up mutual confidence. Like children, they egg each other on, tease each other and hide behind one another. In the absence of another youngster, a growing foal will pester its mother incessantly to play with it and will frequently be rebuffed. In search of another outlet, it will turn to its human companion and see how good at games you are.

It is very tempting to respond to a foal's attempts to tease and play with you, as long as the foal is small and not too strong. Unfortunately, the foal will not forget and will continue to try the same tricks as it grows up, when its hooves planted on your chest might not be so funny and its teeth leave a nasty bruise. Therefore, resist the temptation to allow a young foal to get the better of you, even in fun. Establish from the beginning that you are its leader and it must not take liberties. There is nothing unkind in being consistent about this and the foal will grow up knowing the limits of permissible behaviour and without becoming confused. Ill-mannered older horses are often that way because no one has ever consistently shown them what is permissible and what is not.

Your new foal may be a source of constant fascination, but do not overdo the handling. Remember that foals tire easily and need much of their time just to eat, sleep and grow. A brief lesson in the morning after feeding and another in the afternoon is plenty. If you have more time available spend it just watching from a distance – you will learn a great deal. Many people do not realise, for example, that foals feed frequently but in small amounts, or how many naps they take, or how they respond to the stimuli of their surroundings – people, plants, strange objects, noises, other animals, etc.

Occasionally, a foal is orphaned, either because its mother dies or, rarely, rejects it. If a foster mother cannot be found, there is then no alternative but to rear the foal by hand. Foster mothers can sometimes be arranged via the National Foaling Bank (see Useful Addresses) who will advise on getting the new mare to accept the foal as her own.

This is a skilled task, which usually involves covering the foal with the skin of the mare's own dead foal, carefully introducing the two and holding the mare so that the foal can suckle several times and perhaps over several days. If the mare accepts the foal, she will rear it as her own.

Hand rearing a foal, however, is another proposition altogether and for the first few weeks is very draining, due to the frequency with which the foal needs to be fed. Most foals readily learn to suck a bottle with an appropriate rubber teat and soon progress to drinking their formula from a bucket. The main difficulty, however, is the foal's inclination to become confused about the identity of itself in relation to humans and other horses. Inevitably, it becomes very familiar with the human who feeds it and, as you have to spend a great deal of time with this foal, it is particularly important to keep its behaviour within acceptable parameters. If you do not control its behaviour with the level of discipline that its own mother would have employed, you will have an obstreperous, unmanageable yearling on your hands twelve months later.

Weaning

In simple terms weaning means stopping the foal from suckling. You may find, if you have only the one mare and foal and the mare is not being bred from again, that weaning is not even necessary. The mare will probably wean the youngster herself eventually, although some youngsters will continue to suckle beyond their first year, if allowed to do so! In any event, unless absolutely necessary, it is best not to wean your foal until it reaches at least six months of age. By then it will have received the greatest benefit from its mother's milk in terms of growth and development. It should already be well accustomed to the hay and hard food that will sustain it through the winter, having been fed along with its mother. Mares will often share their feed bowl with their foal initially, and soon you can provide a separate bucket for the foal.

The difficulty of weaning is the anxiety that the forced separation causes both mare and foal, so the main priority is to minimise this. The process is much easier if the foal has companions it already

Breakfast for an orphan foal. The sheepdog acts as guardian and playmate, but the human is in loco parentis and must dispense discipline as well as food.

knows and the simplest method is to remove the mare from the field and put her with other companions of her own in a new field out of earshot of the foal. As long as it has interesting company, the foal soon forgets about suckling and, once the mare's milk has dried up, after a couple of months, mare and foal can live together again, if desired.

If no other companion is available for the foal at home, you must either acquire one, such as a pony or another youngster (make sure it does not have hind shoes on), or make arrangements for your foal to visit companions elsewhere. For example, if you have a friend with a foal which needs weaning, one of you can keep the mares and the other the foals until the weaning process is complete. To wean a foal in isolation is extremely unkind and the stress and loneliness endured may affect its attitude to other horses for the rest of its life.

Chapter 10

The Stallion

The highest priority of the male of any species is to try to ensure the reproduction of his own genes, an aim he pursues with single-minded determination, often at the expense of other males being able to reproduce theirs. This fundamental characteristic is the key reason why humans react to the stallion as they do. Frequently, people's behaviour towards a stallion reflects preconceived but ill-founded notions of the aggressive side of his nature. This leads them to act in an aggressive/defensive way themselves, without ever giving the stallion a chance to behave like a normal horse. Teaching a colt to live harmoniously with humans in the presence of other horses requires patience, tact, skill and, above all, understanding of why the stallion behaves the way he does and how the trainer can inhibit and control his natural inclinations to fit in with a domesticated lifestyle.

Given a mare in season, an entire horse will mate with her if nature is allowed to take its course. Most entires will certainly show an interest and only those which have been consistently trained and handled for work and taught the difference between one kind of work and another will be mentally controlled enough to ignore her and concentrate on what they are being asked to do. If you are going to handle or work a stallion, you need to be aware of the animal's natural behaviour patterns and know how to interpret them and communicate with him effectively, just as you would with any other horse. The only difference with a stallion is that his challenges may be faster and more physical than with a mare or gelding and the consequences of getting it wrong involve a somewhat higher risk of accident or injury to someone. For this reason the entire horse is not a realistic proposition for the inexperienced handler.

The colt with his 'herd'. When it is time to go somewhere, it is the females that lead the way, while the stallion brings up the rear.

ABOVE: *A top Thoroughbred stud. The lifestyle of horses like these denies them not only the chance to run free, but also the companionship of other horses, except for mating purposes.*

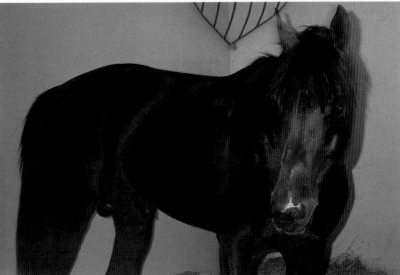

RIGHT: *Life within four walls has varying effects on the temperament of stallions.*

However, the reputation of stallions for being difficult, free with their hooves and teeth, physically overpowering, temperamental and downright dangerous is entirely the product of the unnatural methods most frequently used by people to keep and control them. In the wild, the stallion normally lives with a family 'herd' of a few mares and their offspring of varying ages. In the domestic situation, however, it is difficult, if not impossible, to organise such an arrangement. For ease of management, males that are not required for breeding are castrated in order to minimise the effects of 'male' behaviour. Those retained as entires are frequently kept in total isolation from other horses, forever denied the reassurance of being part of the group, of the pleasures and comfort of touch in the form of mutual grooming and generally of sharing the joys of company. The imposition of such a solitary lifestyle is incredibly stressful for the horse. Apart from the effects of segregation, fear of the horse injuring itself, jumping through fences, escaping, or getting in with mares often results in it being kept unnaturally confined, in its stable, for an unhealthy proportion of its time. Is it any wonder that some stallions, when brought out to be shown off, or to cover mares, spill over with violent energy and frustration. In the larger breeds, such pent up strength and emotion can make the animal very dangerous to handle. Hence the familiar image of the stallion handler with a chifney and a stout stick.

131

The worst scenario occurs where the horses are kept purely for stud work and seldom leave their stables for any other purpose. Often this is because stud owners fear the risk of injury to a valuable horse if it is turned out. Those that are turned out for perhaps an hour each day in a small paddock fare little better as far as mental and physical relaxation is concerned. To keep them in good condition for the stud season, such stallions are often fed appreciable amounts of cereals, a diet that also produces an excessive amount of energy in a horse that is not being ridden. A similar regime of confinement coupled with a high energy diet is also sometimes used for stallions that are shown in hand, with the idea that they will come out bursting with energy and brilliance in the ring. In fact, a horse that has been turned into an unmanageable monster by such treatment seldom shows itself well – there is no substitute for correct, sympathetic training.

Stallions that are ridden regularly, in addition to performing stud duties, are generally much happier animals, even if they are not turned out with company.

Larger racing and performance yards, which may have any number of entires in training, develop routines where the horses can be ridden and handled with the minimum amount of fuss, often going out in groups together for exercise. Basic safety rules are followed, such as staff always wearing hard hats plus body protectors for riding, chifneys used as a matter of course for horses being led in and out from pasture, horses always tied up fairly short for grooming, mucking out and tacking up. Many horses settle to this rather regimented lifestyle with equanimity, although some never do and show their unhappiness in various ways. One may be known as the horse which is difficult to groom, another for trying to bite anyone that passes its stable door, and another for barging out of the stable as soon as the door is opened. In many cases, such problems only start when the horse cannot be worked for some reason and is confined to the stable on box rest. In racing yards populated mainly by young colts, training and stud duties are not combined. Strenuous training often suppresses the development of sexual awareness, especially if fillies are kept in a separate yard, although some colts are less docile than others.

In competition yards, stallions may well be expected to cover mares as well as compete. The advent of artificial insemination (AI) has made the task of combining the two activities much easier, since semen only needs to be collected once from the stallion in order to inseminate several mares. The majority of stallions that are regularly ridden become remarkably calm and manageable, their strength, intelligence and natural presence often enabling them to shine in their chosen field of performance. The rider or handler simply has to remain alert to the fact that the horse *is* a stallion and make sure that it is handled with common sense and mutual respect and given the personal space it needs.

The best of the large establishments we know allows young growing colts to live together in groups until the age of three, with fillies in separate groups. Once backed, before going into regular training, the young horses are still turned out daily, in addition to being ridden, although the colts go out in individual electrically fenced paddocks rather than together.

Rearing the colt

The ideal way to rear a colt is to treat it as much as possible, for as long as possible, like any other young horse. Turned out in a family group, for the first 18 months to 2 years of its life, it will learn the limits of acceptable behaviour from its companions and will not develop any of the abnormal behaviours that result from the stress and boredom of isolation. It will learn discipline from its elders and how to socialise and establish its place in the pecking order with other members of the group. The fact that it is a colt among mares and/or geldings will by no means give it automatic status. Geldings are suitable companions only if the colt has been brought up with them, otherwise fighting may be excessive, especially in the presence of mares. The colt should be handled and given a basic education in exactly the same way as any other youngster (see Chapter 11).

As it begins to become sexually aware, care must be taken in the choice of companions. Its own dam, *provided* she is in foal again, can stay and is a good choice as she will still take the role of disciplinarian when necessary. Alternatively, other young colts or geldings can share the same pasture provided they are well separated from females of mating age. Fit,

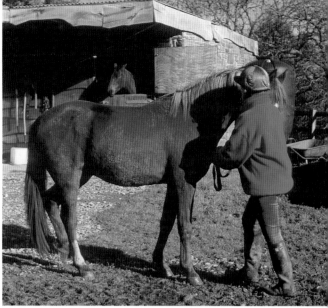

Our three-year-old Arab colt is given his basic education on the yard and expected to pay attention despite the distraction of other horses. Becky asks him to stand while she handles his hind legs.

He learns to back up . . .

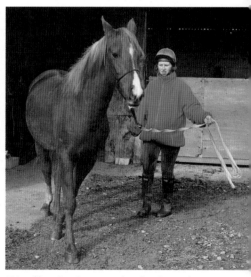

. . . move his forequarters over . . .

. . . and follow with his hindquarters.

Finally, he learns the basics of lungeing. For this 15-minute lesson he was brought in from the field, away from his companions.

elderly horses also make suitable companions and will help control too much exuberance. However, some colts may be too boisterous for old companions that are getting slow and arthritic, so be circumspect and keep a watch on how the group associates with one another. Be aware, also, that a 2-year-old colt may well be capable of covering any fertile mare with which it is turned out. In fact, if it is intended to keep the colt for breeding, running

with an older, experienced mare can be the perfect introduction to mating etiquette.

The colt should be expected to be as well mannered as any other youngster and any tendency to nip or strike out should be firmly stopped (see Chapter 12). The psychological human response of a) expecting bad behaviour and b) allowing the colt to get away with it, just because the animal *is* a colt, must be consciously resisted. If anything, your disciplinary responses must be even quicker and more determined when dealing with a colt, than with a filly or gelding.

You will develop the confidence and experience needed to handle entire males only through familiarity with them and this can be acquired only by working with them under the supervision of someone whose ability you trust.

Riding stallions

The well-educated, properly adjusted stallion is a pleasure to ride. Alert, brave and forward going, his superior physique gives him increased strength and athletic ability, while the intensity of his awareness of his surroundings will make everything seem more vivid and vibrant. To ride a stallion demands your single-minded attention and will raise the level of your ability to 'feel' and 'focus'.

Provided the horse has been treated like a horse and educated with appropriate care and understanding, it should behave in public in most respects like any other horse. However, a stallion is more protective of its personal space than other horses and a red ribbon on its tail is an advisable precaution and a polite way of letting other riders know that your horse is a stallion.

A few stallions find it impossible to suppress sexual behaviour in company, especially towards mares in season and these must be ridden with particular care and restraint. Another rider will not thank you for either the free service, or your

stallion's hooves around their ears. Decreasing the energy level of the feed, increasing the workload and regularity of work and continual repetition of riding out in company will all help towards solving this problem. If such horses are to be ridden, it is advisable not to use them for stud work in the same season until their behaviour settles down.

Handling stud horses

Due to the perceived demand for performance-proven sires, more individual owners are keeping stallions than in former times. The old tradition of the ex-racing Thoroughbred, often put to stud because he failed to succeed as a racehorse and with no other performance criteria to recommend him, might have been sufficient in the past when the show ring or the hunting field was the destiny of the offspring. Today it is no longer seen as a suitable route to improve the quality of youngstock destined for competitive careers. As the demand for competition horses, rather than just riding horses, grows, so the need for stallions that have proved their worth has also grown.

If a horse has succeeded competitively in its own right, you can be fairly sure that it has a good temperament and has been well handled. If it is standing with a non-professional owner you need to check that suitable facilities are available for boarding your mare, if required. The actual covering must be handled in a safe and professional manner

The ridden stallion (right) should behave sensibly and in control in public. The other horse is a mare and the riders are part of the British endurance team, competing abroad.

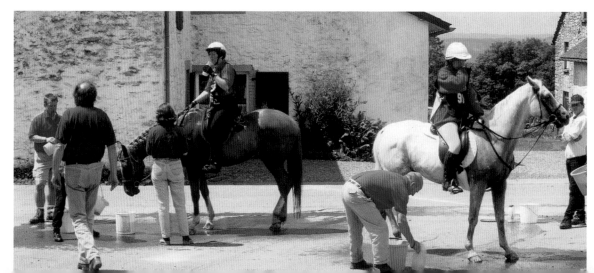

In this photo the mare (second from left) is objecting to lining up with the stallion (left). Mares can initiate trouble as often as stallions do.

and arrangements made with your own or the stallion owner's vet to deal with any fertility problems, treatments and pregnancy diagnosis. Well-run professional studs deal with these aspects as a matter of routine, whereas the single stallion owner may receive only a few visiting mares each year.

Very few owners will permit mares to run with their stallion for fear of injury to the stallion. Running with a stallion can be a useful solution for a mare that is difficult to get in foal, as nature often knows better than the scientists do! Pony stallions, less valuable horses and older stallions are those most likely to be available to run with mares.

Covering in hand is the most frequently used method, where the whole process is under the control of the handlers.

The advantages of the system are:

a) **You know exactly when and whether the mare was covered and there is no doubt as to the identity of the stallion.**
b) **Safety precautions can be taken to prevent the mare from damaging the stallion.**
c) **A teaser can be used to see if a mare is ready before risking a valuable stallion, or exposing him to the stress of courtship without consummation (this can be significant for a stallion that has to cope with a large book of mares during the season and needs to conserve his energy and maintain condition).**

d) **The horses can be separated quickly if need be.**

The disadvantages are:

a) **The mating procedure of horses is noisy, strenuous and often violent, putting handlers at risk from fast-moving, powerful bodies and flying hooves.**
b) **The unnaturalness of in-hand mating is stressful and causes a great deal of anxiety, especially for the mare and particularly if she is restrained by artificial means, such as hobbles or a twitch. The situation is exacerbated if the mare is in heat but not quite ready to mate, when covering can be tantamount to rape!**
c) **Despite the stallion's strong instincts, the forced situation of in-hand covering can have varying effects. Some stallions may be over enthusiastic and try to cover the mare without any preliminaries, making the whole process rushed and frenzied, more dangerous for the handlers and more stressful for the mare. Others, especially if they are expected to cover too many mares, may become disenchanted with the whole business and decline to show any interest.**

Stud stallion management, therefore, is a skilled job involving far more than just bringing out the horse and letting him do what comes naturally.

a) The courtship ritual.

b) The colt prepares to mount the receptive mare.

c) He maintains position by grasping her neck.

d) Dismounting after covering.

e) During covering Rojo's attention has been focused on the mare. Now he is alert for any threats to his supremacy or dangers to his herd.

136

When a stallion is preoccupied with a mare, his attention is distracted from his handler. The handler must therefore allow for this and be prepared to move quickly to stay out of harm's way of both stallion and mare and to still retain control over the stallion. An in-hand bridle, fitted with a stallion chain and leadrein, is normally used for the stallion, although a chifney may be used if extra control is needed. Some studs put the mare in a chifney for covering. Stallions used for both stud and ridden work often learn to differentiate between the tack used for each job and behave accordingly.

To prepare for in-hand covering, the mare's tail is bandaged, to keep it out of the way and her genital area may be washed with disinfectant solution. She will be fitted with 'kicking boots' on her hind feet. These are like thick, felt slippers, designed to minimise any damage to the stallion should she lash out at him. The mare is led up to one side of a 'trying board', which is a solid partition often padded for extra safety. If a teaser is being used (often a quiet older stallion or a pony stallion), he will be led up to the other side and introduced to the mare. Her reaction will be observed. If she continually squeals and lashes out, she is not ready for mating. If she crouches and squirts small amounts of urine, while 'winking' her vulva, then she is ready. Some mares, particularly maiden mares, do both at the same time and the handlers must judge whether the mare is actually ready or not and whether the protest is more than a token one.

If a teaser is not used, then the covering stallion will 'try' the mare. If she is judged ready, the teaser is removed and immediately replaced with the covering stallion, who will sniff the mare and test her scent by curling his lip in the posture known as Flehmen. This action allows the horse to trap scented air in an extra sense organ, called the Jacobson's organ. All horses have this ability, but it is most widely used by stallions when scenting mares. He will continue to sniff, nibble and even bite along her neck and withers until he is fully aroused, working backwards along the trying board. Finally, he is led around behind her and she is moved away from the trying board, so that he can mount and cover her. In some studs it is normal practice for the stallion handler manually to guide the stallion's penis into the mare's vagina. Once positioned, ejaculation takes place rapidly and is signified by the stallion 'flagging' his tail. He may rest for a moment before withdrawing and dismounting. Mare and stallion are then both walked to cool off and to prevent the mare from crouching and urinating and perhaps expelling a quantity of sperm.

Chapter 11

The Young Horse

Initial handling

The value of handling the young foal becomes clear when the bigger, stronger weanling presents itself for further education. If you have bred a foal and given it the lessons described in Chapter 9, you will have a calm, well-mannered youngster to bring on. However, many unhandled weanlings are sold at sales to well-meaning people, who are then faced with the task of winning their confidence and trust and gaining their respect.

A baby foal can be restrained gently but firmly by physical means, with one arm around its chest and the other around its quarters for example. By the time a youngster of even a small breed reaches six months of age, it is too strong and vigorous for that, unless it has been starved and neglected. The experience of going through a sale ring, or even the trip to a new home, also has a disturbing influence and it may be several days before the new arrival settles, particularly if it has just been weaned or separated from companions it has known from birth.

The most effective way to win the trust of a new youngster is to make it dependent upon you. Stable it in a large, airy box with a good bed and be patient. It will soon recognise that you are the source of food and water and look forward to your visits. Spend as much time in the stable as possible, initially without trying to handle it. The aim at this stage is to have the youngster become curious and move towards you, not the other way around.

The 'advance and retreat' method followed by 'join up', as practised by Monty Roberts and others, is based on the principle that it must be the horse's decision to accept the handler rather than the handler dominating the horse by force. Ideally carried out in a 'round pen', the method can be followed in any confined area of suitable size with good footing. The process of winning the horse's confidence is speeded up using 'advance and retreat'. Briefly, this consists of sending the horse away from you around the pen until it shows signs of submission and wanting to stop. These include licking its lips and lowering its head. You then stop sending the horse away, and instead adopt a submissive attitude to encourage the horse to come to you. When it does, 'join up' has been achieved (for more detailed information see Further Reading).

If you do not have such a suitable training area, you will have to be more patient and work in the stable. Curiosity will always get the better of a young horse in the end and you can encourage it by making sure your attitude does not appear threatening. Crouching to put yourself on the same level helps. Avoid looking the youngster in the eye and keep your body outline soft, relaxed and turned sideways to it. Once your touch is accepted, gently and progressively rub all over its body. To begin with, you might only manage to handle the shoulders and

Becky reinforces Mimi's imprint training by handling her ears . . .

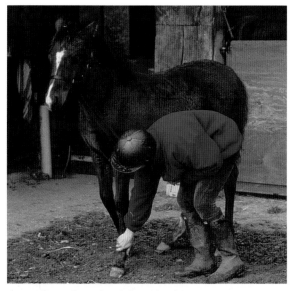

. . . and running a hand down her legs.

chest. Take as many sessions as necessary and do not try to do anything else until the young horse is fully confident in your presence and accepts you moving around it and rubbing all its vulnerable areas – head, back, legs and belly.

Halter breaking

Once this is achieved, it should be relatively easy to slip a headcollar on. Many youngsters are haltered if they are going to be sold, for example, but are not properly trained to lead and tie. Therefore, if you buy a youngster, it is a good idea to repeat the halter breaking and leading process to be sure that it is thoroughly accepted.

This is much the same as described in Chapter 9 for halter breaking a foal. It can be started in the stable where the horse is unable to escape very far. Begin by asking it to move its head laterally in either direction. Pressure on the flank as you gently pull the cheek of the headcollar towards you will encourage it to move its hindquarters over and then its forelegs towards you. Immediately it moves, you must release the pressure, rub and praise the horse and then repeat. This is the beginning of walking on a circle. Progressively, you can encourage the youngster to walk in a circle around you in both directions. The horse learns that by moving towards you it frees itself from pressure. This is the essence of the

leading lesson. As soon as it feels slight pressure on the leadrope, the horse should move towards you. It is vital to realise that if you do not release the pressure the moment the horse moves towards you, it will begin to pull back instead of following. This is the most common mistake made by people trying to teach an exuberant young horse to lead.

Once the horse has learned the lesson in the stable, it can be taken outside. At this stage it is vital to be patient. There are many distractions and the youngster will sample them all, from its companions in the adjoining box to objects on the distant horizon. If you have a big, strong young horse to deal with, it is advisable to use one of the various controller halters on the market, which put pressure on various areas of the face when the horse tries to evade you. It will quickly learn that pulling back, or rushing forwards subjects it to pressure and, provided you are careful never to initiate the pulling, the controller halter will give you more precise control.

A frequent response of a nervous young horse is to plant itself firmly on one spot and refuse to move. This is when the inexperienced handler may resort to pulling and all that happens is that the horse pulls back and may even rear up and go over backwards. Traditional method has it that the handler should carry a whip with which they can reach behind and flick the horse's quarters. This is actually quite difficult to do accurately and can put you in an awkward position relative to the horse should it suddenly leap forwards. A better technique is to go back to asking the horse to move laterally. You may end up moving in the wrong direction, but once movement is achieved you can lead the horse in a circle and then forward again. Sometimes this may have to be repeated a few times, if the horse decides to stop on a particular spot.

Another method, if you have a halter with a long enough leadrope (about 3.6 m (12 ft) is ideal), is to teach the horse to move away from the end of the rope swinging at its quarters. This method can be developed into a series of exercises developed by the American trainer, Pat Parelli. He calls the technique lateral lungeing and explains it fully in his book, *Natural Horsemanship* (see Further Reading).

Once a horse learns to accept being led, it needs to learn how to stop and to stand still when asked. Stopping is achieved by the handler moving fractionally forwards of the leading position and giving a gentle squeeze on the leadrope, at the same time using the voice command 'Whoa' and stopping. If the horse does not stop, the handler is in position to raise a hand in front of the horse's face, which acts as a blocking signal. Horses are usually quick to learn to stop, although the handler should work at achieving a precise transition rather than just having the horse progressively slowing down and falling into the halt.

If your basic handling techniques are effective, it is only one step further to keep the horse's attention on you and have it stand still while you move around it. Remember that a very young horse has a short concentration span and ask it to stand for just a few moments before moving on or doing something else. As your training progresses, the horse can be asked to stand for progressively longer periods. By the time you are ready to introduce the saddle and then to back the horse, it should be capable of standing calmly in an open space while you make all the necessary preparations.

Stable manners

Good stable manners should be developed from the start with any young horse. In Chapter 2 we considered some means of establishing good manners in a horse which had not been adequately conditioned as a youngster. Now we will look at conditioning the responses of the young, untrained horse.

Young horses are eager, enthusiastic and persistent and may not yet have fully accepted the role of the handler as their leader. They may not respect your personal space, especially if they have had little prior handling and are more likely to push, shove and threaten to get to what they want rather than to bite or kick. It is tempting just to push back, for example, to get the feed to the manger, if the youngster is not too big and strong. If this does not work, people often resort to shouting and waving their arms, which may have the desired effect temporarily. Neither attitude will solve the problem long term. Behaviour in the stable should simply reflect a continuation of the methods used to relate to the horse outside, when leading and doing other training work, and the two should be learned simultaneously.

It is important that the youngster learns to accept you entering its stable. Some horses become very protective of the stable as their own private territory at an early age and may try to defend it by threatening behaviour towards anyone entering the box. This is most likely to happen if they feel threatened by their companions, or if they have experienced confusion or mental abuse earlier in their lives. Such behaviour must be firmly discouraged, first by the handler showing their refusal to be intimidated, by squaring up to the youngster and using a deep, growling tone of voice, and, second, by giving a lot of reassurance and reward for good behaviour as soon as it happens.

Swinging the lunge line at the horse's hindquarters to encourage him to move.

a) *The bit can be inserted or, as here, removed by undoing one cheek piece, if the horse is worried about the bridle being passed over its ears.*

b) *These cheek-pieces which clip on to the headcollar are handy for biting youngsters. The headcollar is adjusted to set the bit at the correct height in the youngster's mouth.*

c) *Desert Rose opens her mouth at first, against the unfamiliar feel of the bit. This one is of copper, said to encourage salivation and be warmer than steel.*

d) *Before long, she settles down and accepts this strange new thing.*

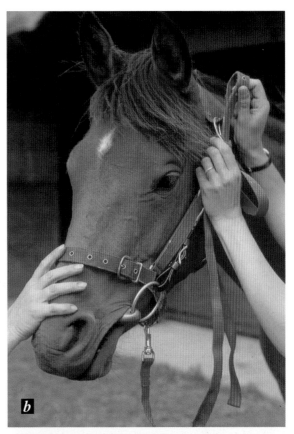

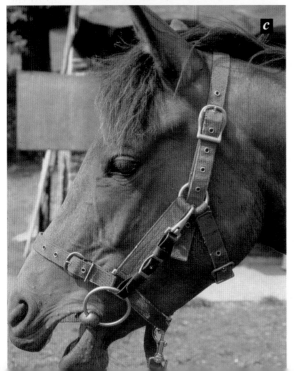

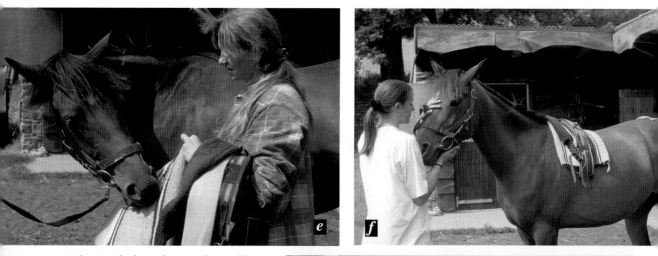

e) *Letting the horse become thoroughly familiar with all its tack goes a long way to dispelling fear or nervousness.*

f) *As Becky passes behind Desert Rose, she keeps her hand over her rump, to let the horse know she is there.*

g) *Doing up the girth gently, one hole at a time.*

Throughout the training of the young horse, praise and, more importantly, pleasurable physical contact, that is, rubbing and stroking, are essential. They let the horse know when it has pleased you and reinforce its inclination to repeat the behaviour that pleased you next time. No aspect of the horse's behaviour is too small or insignificant to warrant you showing your pleasure, even if it is only half a step in the right direction.

The basic lessons a horse needs to learn in the stable are to move back, move over and stand quietly when tied. Backing up is taught early and quite simply by pressure from the fingers on the chest, first one side and then the other, depending on which leg needs to be moved. Start with gentle pressure and increase it until the horse makes a move. The moment it lifts the leg to move back, release the pressure, rub the horse's chest where you were pressing it and praise it warmly. Then repeat several times until the horse responds more quickly. Continue the same

lesson every day. Eventually, you should not need to touch the horse at all – it will learn to move back in anticipation of your body movement.

Moving over is achieved in a similar way with finger pressure on the flanks and your other hand as a restraining influence on the headcollar. You can begin quite far back on the flank, but as the horse's understanding of what you want improves, move your hand farther forwards, until, eventually, you ask it to move over with your fingers behind the girth area where a rider would use their leg. Again, do not forget the reward the moment the horse moves to obey.

Tying up

The loss of freedom of its head is a very worrying situation for a young horse. If it occurs suddenly, without prior habituation, the horse will almost certainly panic, perhaps with fatal results. Therefore tying up must be achieved carefully and progressively. No horse should be tied up until it has learned how to lead properly. Acceptance of the pressure on the headcollar when led will encourage acceptance of the same pressure when tied up. Safety as explained in Chapter 2 must be observed.

The best time for a horse to learn about being tied up is during handling and grooming. The leadrope is initially passed through the tie ring, without actually being tied and with the handler holding the free end. It should be sufficiently long for the handler to move around the horse to the rear without stretching. It should be left loose unless the horse makes a move that tightens it. If the horse has been well trained to lead, it will quickly realise that all it needs to do to slacken the rope and relieve the pressure is to move forwards. If the horse exerts a steady pull, or tries to get away by shaking its head, the handler should remain in place until the horse realises that the way out if its predicament is to move forwards. Only if the horse is at risk through being startled or panicking at the restriction should the handler release the rope, otherwise the lesson is not learned. Panic is only likely if the leading lesson has not been thoroughly absorbed, in which case it should be re-established before you try the tying up lesson again.

When the horse is thoroughly accustomed to moving forwards to relieve pressure on the leadrope, it can be loosely tied with a quick release knot (see Chapter 2). The handler must stay with the horse and be ready to release the rope if necessary. Never leave a young horse tied up alone, even when it seems to have learned the lesson well. Youngsters are always prone to being startled by things happening around them and they forget their lessons when something sufficiently frightening awakens the flight instinct. If they then find themselves restrained, they may well panic and fight the restraint.

Grooming

Ideally young horses should live outside most of the time in a pasture large enough for them to have a gallop and where they can breathe fresh, clean air and strengthen young, growing limbs. Grooming should be kept to a minimum to leave the natural

h) Grooming a hind leg, Becky first runs her hand down the leg to reassure the horse.

i) Fitting brushing boots.

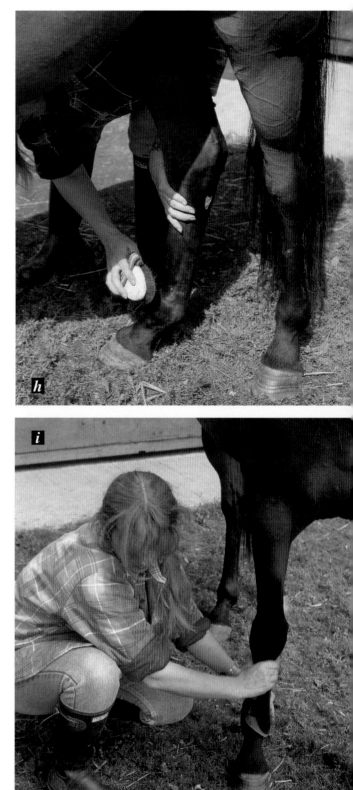

protection in their coats. It should also have regard to the sensitivity of their skin and any ticklish places. Manes and tails can be brushed and tidied but should be left untrimmed unless trimming is essential for showing. The whiskers, ear and fetlock hair should also be left well alone.

Foot trimming

Regular trimming of the feet should be carried out from three months of age and the youngster should be well prepared for the farrier's first visit. If you have bought an older youngster, this training might have been neglected, so picking up the feet should be approached in the same way as for the foal as described in Chapter 9. It might take several days, or even weeks, for the young horse to accept having its feet and legs handled with fuss. The key is to be patient and stay calm, progressively rubbing your hands up and down its legs. It is a natural reaction to drop the leg and move back if the horse jerks its leg away from your hands. Instead, try to keep your hands on the leg, without trying to hold it, until the horse puts it down and stands quietly. In this way the horse will discover that jerking away does not have the result it expected and it will become desensitised and accept your touch on this vulnerable part of its body more quickly.

When it is comfortable with you rubbing its cannons and fetlocks, you can ask the horse to pick up its foot (see Chapter 3). At first just pick it up and let the horse put it down again immediately. Gradually, you can hold the foot up for longer. The same process must be followed for each leg in turn. Once the horse is happy to pick up its feet when requested, you can proceed to tapping the hooves gently to simulate the hammering in of nails when the horse is shod. Do not stop if the horse snatches its foot away. The object of the exercise is to continue until the horse *stops* snatching away, that is, to 'desensitise' it to the feeling so that it accepts it as safe and normal. Desensitisation is the basis of much of the early training of the young horse.

When the farrier arrives to trim its feet, the youngster has to contend with several new things other than just picking its feet up, not least of which is meeting and accepting another new person. A good farrier will be patient with a youngster. He will allow it a little time to get to know him, will stay calm and quiet and make allowances for fidgeting and nervousness. However, it is not his job to train it for you and he needs a basically well-handled animal, as well as a safe, clean, clear space to work in, if he is to do a good job of trimming its feet.

Introducing tack

There are no rules that govern the right age to introduce items of tack, such as bridles, bits, surcingles, etc. Frequently, young horses are not bitted until just before backing and too many tender young mouths are spoilt by inconsiderate use of the hands, particularly on the ground.

Many professional horse trainers, working in a traditional way, introduce each new piece of tack or aspect of education as soon as the horse tolerates the previous one. This is not entirely the trainer's fault, since owners often expect to send them a virtually unhandled 3-year-old and have it returned, with its basic schooling completed and ready to ride away, within an average of about six weeks. The result is that the horse has learnt the bare minimum and is

Inquisitive as ever, Desert Rose has a good sniff at the lunge lines. Becky is convinced that the three-year-old filly 'has been here before'.

This lesson is a reminder of the long reining she learned last year.

Becky has dispensed with Vicky's assistance and taken the youngster for a walk in the country.

behaving in a tolerably acceptable way because it has been in the hands of a professional who knows how far they can push their luck. Such a horse, returned to a less experienced owner, is often a problem waiting to happen. Frequently, it ends up back with the trainer, or another trainer, within a few weeks or months because it has become unmanageable or unrideable. Ultimately, it costs the owner more money than if time had been allowed to do the job properly in the first place. A word of advice here if you are sending a young horse to a professional to be backed or brought on. Before you take the horse back, have a course of at least six to ten lessons with the trainer and your horse. In that way any potential difficulties can be nipped in the bud and you and the horse can become accustomed to each other with an experienced person, who already knows the horse, on hand to help you. This investment will repay you many times over in your future partnership with your new horse.

Even if you decide to send your youngster away for actual backing and initial ridden work, there is an almost unlimited amount that you can do at home in preparation that will make the professional's task easier and more quickly accomplished. All the handling procedures we have previously discussed count towards this and you can also accustom the horse to tack.

There are many theories about the best means of bitting. The traditional method was to fit a mouthing bit with keys and let the horse get used to it, playing with the keys to encourage salivation, before introducing the ordinary snaffle for lungeing and backing. We have not found this necessary and always begin with a simple, mullen-mouth rubber snaffle, or, if the horse has a small mouth and finds this too thick, a happy-mouth jointed or 'peanut' snaffle.

Introducing the bridle poses two problems: getting the bit into the horse's mouth and getting

145

the bridle over the horse's head. The first is made easier if the horse has been subjected previously to desensitisation of its mouth. This should be done with all horses in any case to make the vet's job easier when he needs to examine the mouth or rasp the teeth. Tellington touch techniques of massaging the lips and gums are very useful in this as the horse soon learns to enjoy the sensation. Desensitisation of the mouth is also one of the techniques used in foal imprinting (see Chapter 9).

Before you begin, make sure the bridle is adjusted to sufficient length and remove the noseband. We prefer to work with the youngster in the stable untied and put the bridle on over the headcollar or halter.

We use the following procedure:

- **Show the bridle to the horse and let it have a good sniff.**
- **When it loses interest, take the bridle cheeks in your right hand and the bit in the palm of your left, as you stand beside the horse at its left shoulder.**
- **Step quietly up to its head and slip your right hand under the jaw and gently over the nose on the far side. Do not try to hold the nose down.**
- **Slide your left thumb into the horse's mouth and, if necessary, wiggle it against the palate to encourage the horse to open its mouth. The moment it does so, slip the bit in.**
- **Be prepared for the horse to raise its head to try to get away from the bit and just go with the movement.**
- **When the horse relaxes, ease the headpiece over the ears, being careful not to squash or pull on them. Some horses which are perfectly happy to have their ears and polls groomed choose this time to decide you cannot possibly touch them there. In this case, undo the cheek piece from the headpiece, so that the headpiece can be lifted over the ears like a headcollar strap, then do up the cheek piece. If you are not sure of your horse's reaction, it is probably best to be prepared for this and begin with the cheek piece already unbuckled.**
- **Great care must be taken to avoid catching the youngster's teeth with the bit when bridling and unbridling.**

- **At first we leave the bridle on for ten minutes each day. The time is increased gradually, while the youngster is having its lessons.**
- **Other tack is introduced in turn, always following the same procedure of showing it to the young horse and allowing it to become thoroughly used to it before fitting.**

A common error made by inexperienced handlers is to concentrate on the goal rather than the process. For example, let us assume that you have

Backing Merlin for the first time, I lean over his back from a mounting block, while Becky reassures him.

He doesn't mind the weight on his back, so Becky leads him around the yard in both directions.

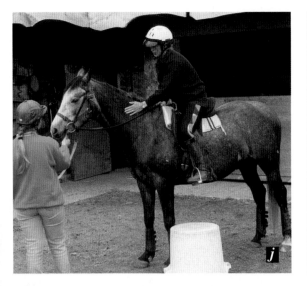

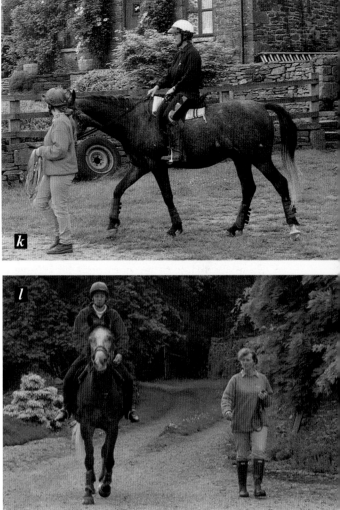

j) The next step, again from the mounting block is to quietly swing a leg over his back and sit up. He stands with his legs slightly splayed to support the unfamiliar weight.

k) Becky leads him quietly around again. Backing should be this simple.

l) A couple of days later, he is walking confidently along the drive, with Becky on the ground beside him.

accustomed the horse to stand still while you handle its legs. Then you decide that it is time to introduce brushing boots. Your goal is to get the boots on so the horse can get used to wearing them. However, you find it starts to move around when you try to do up the first boot. To the horse, the boots are a totally new and different situation. Just because it stands still for you to groom its legs, does not mean it will do so while you attach what could be a dangerous trap to each one. It is no use getting impatient with the horse and ordering it to stand. You must take time for it to become familiar with the boots and convinced they will not harm it.

Similarly, to accustom the horse to a saddle pad or blanket, do not immediately try to put it on the horse's back whilst making nervous-sounding, soothing noises. That tells the horse this is dangerous! Instead, show the blanket to the horse. Let it see and sniff it all over. Quietly rub its neck and shoulders with it. Shake it a bit. Increase your movements until you can wave it in the air and sling it over the horse's withers without any fearful reaction. Take several sessions to do this.

Do not let the small goal of 'putting on the saddle blanket' or the larger one of 'backing the horse' get in the way of the learning process. If you hurry the latter, you will end up with a horse which just about tolerates what humans do and may eventually become inured to the routine, but will never really accept it nor develop the trust on which you can build a true partnership.

Once the saddle blanket is accepted, there will be no difficulty in putting the breaking roller over the horse's back. The benefit of thoroughly desensitising the horse to having its body touched all over, including the girth area, becomes apparent when you want to fasten a girth for the first time. The horse should not be nervous and the only new

147

It isn't all that easy. A few weeks later, resistance to the bit develops during basic schooling. Erupting teeth are the problem and we solve it by riding him in a bitless bridle, until his teeth settle down.

Elf has also been backed and is introduced to interesting things in a nearby arena.

thing it has to accept now is the slight pressure and feel of the girth itself. At first, fasten it just enough to close around the horse's belly and stay in place without tension. Then fasten the breastplate and lead the horse around the stable or working area to get used to the feeling. Remember, a breastplate must always be used with a roller to prevent the risk of it slipping back. Over two or three sessions, the girth can be gradually tightened to a safe working tension, but be careful not to fasten it so tightly that the horse is uncomfortable. An over-tight girth can restrict the horse's breathing and movement and even cause muscle ruptures.

By the time you want to introduce the saddle, the horse is already used to things on its back and to being girthed up. However, the saddle is a larger, heavier item, so give the horse plenty of opportunity to get used to it before putting it on. Ideally, place it somewhere in front of the horse so it can look at it, smell it and walk round and view it from all angles to reassure itself that there is nothing to fear. Pick it up, flap it up and down, turn it over and generally show the horse that this is just another boring piece of equipment. Putting it on should not be a problem either, since the horse is already used to things above its back.

Apply the same principle of small, thorough, progressive steps to everything that you introduce to the young horse and preparation for backing should be fun, interesting and trouble free.

Ground work

Lessons with a young horse need to be kept short to avoid boredom – 10–20 minutes is usually enough. They need to be varied as the youngster will learn quickly and soon start thinking up ways to avoid doing what you want. The handler must be totally consistent and reasonable in the demands made. It will not work if you are in a bad mood and shout at the horse one day, then allow boisterous behaviour the next. Your cues or aids must be clear, precise and the same each time, whether you are using finger pressure, your voice, or artificial aids such as the halter rope, lunge line or whip. The latter can be used to guide, control and encourage, but must never be used to punish.

The horse does not understand the concept of punishment in the same way that humans do. It simply learns that if it does a certain thing, an unpleasant consequence will ensue. It only makes the connection between the two if the unpleasant consequence (usually a verbal reprimand, a bump or a slap) occurs almost simultaneously with the 'bad' behaviour. This is why using a whip to punish a horse is futile. By the time you have raised it, you are already too late.

People's eagerness to get on and ride often results in the horse's training on the ground being cut short, especially if the horse is already a 3-year-old. This is a shame as your partnership with a horse can develop through playing ground games, starting with the weanling and continuing throughout its life.

Use your imagination to find different things to do. The scope of these games is limited only by the physical capabilities of the horse. For example, young horses should not be asked to do anything that puts excessive strain on their limbs or joints. There is no space in this book to go into ground games in detail, but see Further Reading for more information.

Backing

People often magnify the prospect of backing the youngster out of all proportion. If the preparation has been done thoroughly and correctly, backing is just another step in a continuing process, which the young horse will accept without fear or violent reaction. From putting your arm around the foal to acclimating the 3-year-old to someone standing above it on a mounting block, everything except actually sitting on the horse can be done to show it that there is nothing to fear. By now, the horse should also be well accustomed to the bit and, ideally, to the feel of rein aids through being long reined. Nearly all the problems that occur with backing young horses happen because the preparatory work has been rushed or neglected.

When we are ready to back a youngster we begin with a short lesson to give it a chance to work off any exuberance if necessary, for example, on the

Within a few weeks her basic flatwork is progressing well.

lunge, and to get it settled and paying attention. It is already well used to wearing the saddle and the feel of the stirrup irons flapping against its sides. It is also used to standing still quietly when asked. We always have two people on hand, one to mount the horse and the other to control it as necessary. The bridle is fitted over the halter so that the horse can be led or the rider can exert some control without over use of the reins.

The horse is led alongside a mounting block in familiar surroundings in the yard – an arena would be better – and is stopped beside the mounting block. The handler stands in front of the horse, facing it to prevent any inclination to forward movement before the rider is ready, and holding the leadrope, but loosely. If you take a firm grasp on the leadrope, the horse will inevitably move. A basic rule when handling horses is that when the horse is doing what you want it to do, you do nothing.

The rider steps up on to the mounting block – remember, the horse is already happy this far. The rider repeats previous lessons of leaning over the horse's back, patting and stroking its shoulder and flank and then, lifting their feet from the block, the rider leans over and distributes their weight evenly over both sides of the horse. The horse should be allowed to stand for a moment or two to become accustomed to the unfamiliar weight and the patting and stroking is repeated.

The handler next asks the horse to walk forwards in the normal way, at first just a few steps and then in a small circle, halting at the mounting block. The rider regains their feet and after a minute or two, the exercise is repeated, circling in the opposite direction. If the horse is hesitant or disturbed, we will leave it there and repeat the next day until the horse is calm and stops worrying. If the horse is relaxed and happy, we will proceed to the next step.

This time the rider puts their foot in the stirrup, still working from the mounting block and, taking most of their weight on their hands, brings the other foot up so that they are standing up straight, ready to take their leg over the horse's back. Some horses will step forwards or sideways at the unfamiliarity of weight on one side, so be prepared for this and stay relaxed. The rider then leans forwards over the horse's neck and carefully lifts their straight leg clear over the horse's back. They wait for a moment to let the horse get used to their presence in that position and continue stroking the horse before slowly straightening up. The horse should be allowed to relax for a moment or two before leading it forwards as before and circling on both reins with a pause in between. You should appreciate that being asked to move with this new weight on its back forces the horse to balance itself differently and is initially very tiring.

Over the next few days we repeat the backing process, gradually asking the horse to walk farther and mounting and dismounting from both sides, but still using the mounting block. By the third or fourth session, the rider is co-ordinating aids from the saddle, particularly the legs, with those of the handler on the ground. Once the horse begins to respond to the rider's aids, the handler is dispensed with and the horse is ridden independently. Since the horse is still uncoordinated under the rider's weight, we introduce rein aids gradually, co-ordinating them with what the horse already understands of nose pressure from the halter.

From this point on the horse's basic ridden education can begin. An arena with a good ground surface is essential for basic schooling to develop the horse's musculature and suppleness and its ability to balance itself and work towards self-carriage. If you do not have one, it is worth hiring one to make progress with this work. In any case, even the most accomplished riders benefit from regular instruction and beginning the training of a new young horse is an ideal incentive.

Apart from arena work, which should be done judiciously, having regard to the horse's physical growth and development, short hacks help develop confidence and also build up strength. These need to be educational, at first in company and then alone. You should pay attention to your riding, to allowing the movement of the horse under you and to staying balanced. Trotting for short distances on the flat or up slight inclines can be introduced quite soon, but only for short distances and provided the rider is balanced. So-called 'pullers' are often created by riders who allow young horses to run on at a flat out trot or canter before they have developed the strength to balance themselves at the faster paces and before they have learned obedience to the correctly applied aids.

The golden rule with training any young horse is that if things are getting out of control, you go back as many steps as necessary to re-establish the proper relationship of the horse respecting you as its leader.

Young horses often follow the same pattern of progress. At first, they are calm and obedient when ridden. Everything is new and strange and they rely heavily on you for reassurance. However, as their strength and confidence develop, they depend on you less. Sooner or later they decide they do not want to do what you ask, whether in the school or out on a hack. This is the first test of the success of your prior training and conditioning. You should be in tune with the horse, and concentrating fully on the present moment. In that case, all that may be necessary for the horse to relax and return to attentiveness and obedience is a slight shift of your weight, a squeeze of leg or rein, or a reassuring word or pat.

Leading the two youngsters home after a summer evening ride.

Chapter 12

The Problem Horse

Problem horse or problem owner?

It has to be said that nearly all horse problems are rooted in either the current owner/handler, or someone who has handled the horse in the past, not in the horse itself. In earlier chapters we considered the nature of the horse and how it perceives the world and reacts to it. We went on to discover how we can help the horse to learn by taking its natural inclinations into account and using them to help it understand what we want it to do.

Many people do their best to follow this basis of developing a partnership with their horse – until something goes wrong. Then they forget all about the horse's natural behaviour and psychology and try to exert discipline in a purely human framework. The situation is even worse if the horse has frightened them, and made them nervous. In the average, normally caring owner, shouting, rough treatment via the reins or leadrein, stick waving and punishment with the whip are more likely to be the result of the handler's frustration, fear, and lack of knowledge of what else to do rather than straightforward aggressiveness towards the horse. The latter may occur, through ignorance, in some situations and communities, but such handlers are unlikely to be reading this book, although we should be aware of the possibility of having to handle a horse that has a past history of rough treatment.

A badly treated horse or pony, in our experience, is more likely to be cowed and fearful of humans than difficult to handle. The problems displayed by such horses might include being difficult to catch, showing signs of aggression in the stable when the handler comes to invade their 'safe' space, and nervousness about being groomed shown by an inclination to nip or cow kick. All kinds of problems can occur when the horse is ridden, due to its fear of being roughly treated and attempts to put an end to its pain. A horse with such problems is not a project for an amateur. Its rehabilitation is a long-term, skilled job, requiring the slow and painstaking development of trust and co-operation. Even then, the horse will never entirely forget its past.

Fortunately, most of the horses you will meet in riding centres, or being sold through reputable sources, do not fall into this unlucky category and any problems you have to deal with are those which develop between you and the horse in the course of your partnership, still coloured, of course, by the horse's previous experiences.

When a problem occurs, it is essential to understand the cause, even if you had to deal with it first and work out the reason afterwards. The majority of behavioural problems can be resolved, minimised or even prevented by your anticipation of what the horse might do and the speed of your reaction.

Let us look at a variety of problems, their causes, how to cope with them and how to help the horse learn that such behaviour is unacceptable. Whenever you are schooling a problem horse, remember to take appropriate safety precautions and wear suitable clothing, including a safety helmet, gloves and sensible footwear.

Biting

Cause

The horse uses its mouth in many ways that we humans use our hands – to scratch an itch, to slap away an irritation such as a fly or a tickling grooming brush, to warn or drive away something or someone that is annoying it, to explore the texture of something (and at the same time to smell or taste it). In the case of a young colt, nipping is a way of testing things out and attempting to assert its authority over them. If it nips another youngster, the other will either retaliate or run away, in either case

Biting develops from natural behaviour. This youngster wants the older horse to play.

a play-fight can be initiated. If it nips its dam or an older horse, it will probably be severely chastised – the older horse laying back its ears, baring its teeth and lungeing at the youngster, actions which firmly say 'Do that again and you're in trouble!' This is usually a sufficient deterrent. This dominant, older horse behaviour is also the key to how the human handler can deter a horse from unwarranted biting.

Before we look at the cure, however, we must see whether the horse has any justification for biting. It commonly occurs when the horse is being groomed, girthed up, or having rugs fitted or removed and the most obvious cause is that these actions are hurting, or at least irritating the horse in some way. If the problem is not ingrained, removing the cause, by doing the tasks more carefully, will often put an end to the biting.

Solving the problem

Biting hurts. If you habitually hurt your horse when tacking up or grooming, he is perfectly justified in hurting you back, so take care not to pinch or bruise sensitive skin and adjust the girth one hole at a time, evenly on both sides. If you take every precaution and your horse still bites, that is unacceptable behaviour. Tying it up short, so that it cannot reach you, is often suggested, but that does not cure the problem although it might prevent it. Having to tie the horse up short all the time is also a confrontational act in that it artificially restricts the

horse by making it uncomfortable and forcing rather than inviting its co-operation.

When a horse really bites you without justification, the answer is to reply swiftly as a more dominant horse would reply. Immediately face towards it, stepping right up to it in a strongly threatening way and bump it hard on the neck, chest or shoulder, at the same time using your voice in a deep, threatening, growling tone. The idea is to alarm the horse with your retaliatory threat so that it reacts with submission, so do not step back until the horse steps away from you. (Some unenlightened people advocate hitting the horse on the nose. Do not do this – it will just make the horse head-shy. Others suggest biting back, but you will probably be too slow for the horse to grasp the significance and end up with a mouthful of hair and a confused horse.)

Be aware that a serious biter may not give up after one try and be ready to reprimand in the same way as soon as it makes another move towards biting you. Carried out correctly, this approach always works.

Horses are often more inclined to offer to bite you, by swinging their heads towards you with their ears back, than to actually carry through the threat with their teeth. If they habitually do this for no good reason, a sharp, quick elbow in their way will soon deter them. The same applies to young colts that nip in play and boisterousness rather than for any other reason.

Whenever a horse reacts positively to any reprimand (e.g., by stepping back or desisting from its offer to bite in the above two cases), it must immediately be followed up by reassurance and praise. You want to cure the problem, not make the horse afraid of you. The reward for the correct response to your reprimand will give the horse back its confidence and also reinforce its inclination to make the right response.

Barging

Cause
Barging is a habit of strong horses that have never been taught stable manners and respect for their owners. It can be quite dangerous, since a horse that has learned that it can control its handler by means of its sheer size and strength might develop the habit as a resistance in other ways, for example, by squashing you against the stable wall.

Solving the problem
As we know, respect is the absolute key to the horse/human relationship, so obtain respect and you will cure the barging. The horse that barges in the stable almost certainly also does so outside and both problems must be addressed. Solving the latter will help solve the former.

Traditionally, horses which are unmanageable to lead are put in a bridle for more 'control'. Unfortunately, this puts a considerable amount of pressure on the horse's mouth. A much better solution is to use a controller halter, such as the 'be nice' halter, which tightens and puts pressure on the poll when the horse misbehaves. The instructions for correct fitting and use which come with the halter must be followed. A long leadrope, ideally about 3.6 m (12 ft) is also needed. If the horse is really strong or disobedient, the longer leadrope gives you leeway for stopping the horse when it might have got away from you on a shorter rope.

The solution is to re-train the horse to lead obediently in hand, going right back to basics. An arena or enclosed yard is the ideal place. In re-training a horse, your reactions must be even quicker than with an unschooled youngster. You must think one step ahead and be ready for whatever the horse might do. Ask the horse to walk on in the normal way, keeping yourself slightly in front of its shoulder. The bargy horse inevitably charges ahead and as it reaches the end of the slack on the leadrope, give a sharp tug, to bring it up short and turn it towards you. The controller halter will reinforce your action. Do not let yourself become involved in a steadily increasing pull. Keep walking and ask the horse to walk on again.

Rafiki wants attention too. The raised head shows that he is being persistent and trying to assert himself over Becky.

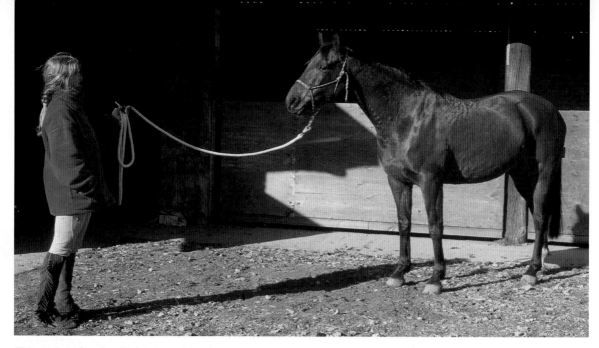

Tammy is inclined to lack respect for others' personal space. Becky is showing her how to be more aware of her own space and that of others too.

The lowered head is a sign of submission as Becky asks Tammy to move around her in a circle.

Consistent voice commands, delivered in a calm, neutral tone, will help and will also assist in reminding you to be completely consistent in your actions. Whenever the horse walks calmly and correctly beside you, praise it quietly.

Continue the process as long as necessary, bringing the horse to a sharp halt every time it gets ahead of the required position beside you. Walking on a circle will be less tiring for you. Once the horse begins to get the idea, practise halting and moving off again. Eventually, repeat the whole process leading from the other side, on a circle to the right. You will probably find the horse reverts to barging off at first.

154

Ria is trying to barge Becky with her shoulder in order to get to the foals.

This may be a tedious process, but frankly, if you do not have the necessary patience, training horses is not for you. These lessons will have to be reinforced several times, as the horse which adopts this type of behaviour is unlikely to learn complete respect for some time.

A horse which barges into you whilst being led has a slightly different problem in that physical contact is the horse's way of seeking reassurance. This horse needs to learn confidence in its ability to move forwards on its own and to control its own body. Long reining is the ideal solution to this problem. As part of this process time should be spent practising normal leading so that the horse learns to walk quietly beside you on a loose lead rein without being pulled and without pushing into you. Again, this can be taught on a circle, using the same principles as for teaching a horse to lunge, and a long leadrope is handy to flick at the horse's quarters to encourage it forwards from behind rather than pulling on the leadrope.

Barging in the stable should improve as the outdoor leading lessons progress, but, meanwhile, should not be tolerated. When you open the door to enter the stable, insist that the horse stands back. Face the horse squarely and use the butt end of a whip to push against its chest until it moves back. If it ignores this amount of pressure, use something a little sharper, for example, a blunt spur, to get the horse's attention. Use your voice, deeply and warningly. Immediately the horse begins to step back, reward it with praise and rubbing its chest. If it barges forwards, repeat the exercise. Put a halter on this type of horse whenever you are working with it in the stable and insist that it keeps its attention on you. Tie it up if you need to move around it, not too short, but just so that it cannot trample over you as though you were not even there. Whatever you are doing – skipping out, filling the hayrack – keep your attention on the horse. Keep talking to it. The more time you can spend working with this horse, the better. Use massage techniques to increase its awareness of its own body and of you moving around it. Practise getting and keeping its attention. Ultimately, it will learn that whenever you are in its vicinity, it must respect your presence and your space.

Kicking: cow kick

Types of kick and the reasons for them were described in Chapter 2 and the method of coping when a ridden horse kicks out in Chapter 8.

The kick threat. Ria has flexed her hocks, ready to lash out.

Cause

Horses rarely make a habit of kicking out at their handlers on the ground unless there is a persistent irritation, such as thoughtless grooming. The most likely occasion for a cow kick is when you are trying to do something that the horse knows is unpleasant, such as dressing a minor wound on a leg. In most cases the horse will lift the leg and wave it in the air rather than seriously trying to kick you. If seriously disturbed, it may put more force and speed behind the action.

Solving the problem

The usual retaliatory return threat, as though you were another horse, is normally sufficient. In this situation, it takes the form of squaring up to the horse's rear, giving a hard smack or bang on the quarters and using a strong, deep voice of reprimand. This is often enough to prevent a re-occurrence.

If the horse habitually cow kicks, you must find the reason and remove it, then gradually convince the horse that the irritation has gone.

Kicking: striking out

Cause

Horses strike out, sometimes combining the action with a rear, when they are over excited and trying to evade the handler's control. Youngsters are the most frequent culprits, before they have learnt complete respect.

Solving the problem

The youngster that strikes out must be dealt with firmly, using the same principles of retaliatory threat and combining a sharp tug on the leadrope, adopting a threatening posture and using your voice. A controller halter is useful if the horse is inclined to combine the action with a rear. The main concern of the handler is to keep out of the way of flying hooves while reprimanding the horse. A smack on the chest or belly with a stick will help, but only if you can do so safely and quickly while the horse is still in the act of striking or rearing. With this problem, your reaction must not be half-hearted. The horse must be left in no doubt that its behaviour is unacceptable. Once the horse is standing four-square again, ask it to come alongside you and then praise it before leading it on.

Kicking: lashing out

Cause

Horses may kick out behind at various threats, usually when being ridden, but the most common are other horses and dogs. Any horse may kick out when startled, but the biggest danger is the horse that habitually kicks out as a warning to anything invading its space from the rear.

Solving the problem

This habit must be broken, or someone will eventually be hurt. If the horse is moving on at a good pace when it kicks out, the remedy is to give it one good smack with the whip and, at the same time, drive it forwards with plenty of leg and a verbal reprimand. Take care, however, that using the whip will not increase the risk of the person or horse behind you being kicked if the horse lashes out again and only do so if it is safe.

If the horse is in a narrow space, immediately use your leg and seat strongly to turn its quarters away from other horses or people, at the same time as giving a verbal reprimand. A smack is a useful deterrent for kickers, but only if given quickly enough and only if it does not increase the risk to others. As soon as it is safe to do so, ride the horse strongly forwards.

Horses misbehave when the rider's attention is elsewhere, even momentarily. If you are aware that the horse you are riding is inclined to kick out at others, the best means of prevention is to see that it is never in a position to do so. Warn companions to keep their distance if they get too close and keep your horse moving forwards on a contact. Concentrate on riding, not on chatting or looking at the scenery with your horse on a loose rein. At a halt, for example, to go through a gate, turn the horse's quarters away from its companions. The more you concentrate on the horse, get it into the habit of listening to you and moving forwards when asked, the less likely it is to even think about kicking.

Spooking and shying

Cause

Shying is the horse's method of getting away from something it spots that might be dangerous and, at the same time, putting itself in a position to have a good look and see how dangerous it really is. It most often happens when the horse is moving on at a trot or canter. At the walk it may happen when something near it makes an unexpected, sudden move, for example, a plastic bag caught in a gust of wind. The shy may be a half step sideways and a bend, so that the horse can focus clearly on the offending object, or it might be a huge leap that may or may not unseat the rider.

Solving the problem

Reprimanding a horse for shying does not solve the problem and may even reinforce the horse's inclination

Merlin's yawn is a reaction to the stress of losing the argument with Ria.

The horse is feeling skittish and has shied off to the left. To deal with shying, sit deep and ride the horse forward.

157

to shy next time, as it thinks 'Gosh, my rider reacted too, so that thing must have been dangerous!'

Younger horses are more inclined to shy for genuine reasons than older, more confident ones. The latter, when feeling fit and fresh, may shy out of exuberance and if this becomes an habitual problem, less food and more work is the answer.

Shying out of genuine worry or nervousness needs a different approach. Remember, the rider is the 'herd leader' and the dominant member of the partnership, or should be. Your riding technique and presence on its back must give the horse confidence so that it does not feel the need to shy. Let us look at two scenarios.

A plastic bag is caught on a bush in a narrow lane and is flapping in the breeze. Your horse spots it from a distance and you feel it tense up. This alerts you to the fact that your horse is going to do something, so you tense up too. The horse feels your tension and thinks 'Oh help, my rider is worried, so that thing must be dangerous.' The next thing you know, you are facing in the opposite direction and lucky to still be in the saddle.

Now imagine the same scenario. The horse spots the bag, but you are sitting balanced and at ease on its back, breathing deeply and calmly and maybe whistling a tune. Your legs are softly on the horse's sides and your hands have a light, but even contact on the reins, holding them softly, not hanging on for dear life! The horse may be worried, but is aware that you are not, so it continues on its way. As it gets close it can see the plastic bag is scary but not really threatening and it continues past, maybe with hesitation followed by a little scurry, but still trusting you. As your partnership develops and its confidence increases, such things will be progressively less of a problem.

Shying often happens much more quickly than that. The secret is to be aware and ready for it without letting yourself be tense. If you are correctly positioned it is easy to ride a horse forwards when you sense a slight hesitation, but the most important means of prevention is to keep your seat softly in the saddle – as soon as you start to tense up, your seat inevitably comes off the saddle, allowing the horse's hind quarters to escape you. If the shy is a big one, you are much more likely to stay on board if you are in a good riding position

than if you are tense and crouching.

Sometimes, on an older horse, you can spot an object yards ahead and know full well that your horse is working up a plan to shy. A slight pressure of your seat and legs may be all that is needed to change its mind.

Napping

Cause

Whereas shying is usually a spontaneous reaction to a perceived danger, napping may have many causes and the place and situation in which it occurs will often give the clue to the reason.

Horses will often nap in exactly the same place, for example, a road turning away from home. Others nap at certain objects, or when asked to do something, such as a particular school exercise or jump.

Napping, is when the horse balks and refuses to go forward, as shown here by the raised head and unco-operative expression.

Solving the problem

The cause must be diagnosed before you can effect a cure. Is the horse in pain? For example, does it refuse to jump because it has a problem that will cause it pain on landing. If so, the physical problem must be resolved before you can tackle the behavioural one. Pain may have a variety of causes, many of which may not be very evident, so a thorough examination should be made by your vet. Teeth, feet, legs and back are all potential problem sites.

Confusion is another cause of napping. The horse does not understand what you want, so rather than go forwards it simply puts the brakes on and refuses to go at all. It may go backwards or twist and turn to evade the rider. This, obviously, is a rider problem and if the rider is inexperienced, a sympathetic instructor is needed to sort things out.

Fear is often the cause in a young horse that lacks confidence in going out alone. Such a horse will often try to tuck itself in behind a companion if riding out in company rather than go alongside or in front. Attempting to beat the horse past the feared obstacle will not help and will probably just make it more reluctant next time. Some riders resort to getting off and leading the horse past the trouble. This will help to give the horse confidence, but may not mean that you will be able to ride past another time.

Ideally, horses that nap through fear should receive more basic schooling and should be hacked out in company, gradually being encouraged to take the lead for a while until their confidence improves. If the horse naps at something when ridden out alone, the rider should keep their seat firmly and softly in the saddle, their legs on and an even contact on the reins. Your seat and legs ensure that the horse goes forwards under your control, while maintaining a contact gives the horse more confidence and awareness that you are still there and in charge. Beginners often throw the reins away when a horse naps, thinking that it will be more inclined to go forwards on a loose rein. This is not the case and merely gives the horse the opportunity to turn away from the feared object.

Staying calm, relaxed and continuing to ride the horse forwards should eventually convince it that there is nothing to fear and it will pass the worrying obstacle. For more on encouraging a horse to cope with strange obstacles, see Chapter 7.

Occasionally, horses nap out of naughtiness, stubbornness and basic lack of respect for the rider. They do not want to go somewhere so they put the brakes on. Occasionally, there is the horse that will never go past a certain distance from home or even leave the yard, or turns and makes for home at a particular point when ridden out. This is a case of a mismatch between a disrespectful, poorly trained horse and an inexperienced, often nervous rider. The horse needs to be re-trained by someone more experienced and the rider to have some lessons on a more obliging mount.

Bucking

Cause

Horses buck for two reasons: in fun and high spirits, or because something about being ridden is seriously bothering them and bucking is one way to try to get rid of the aggravation. The problem with both kinds of bucking is that it can become habitual. In the first case the horse may take to bucking whenever it starts out on a ride as a way of releasing pent up energy. In the second case, the horse may have learned, even when the cause is removed, that bucking is a good way of avoiding a less experienced rider's aids.

Solving the problem

The horse that bucks in exuberance finds the process enjoyable and is therefore inclined to do it again unless something puts it off the idea.

Experienced riders are usually aware if a horse is about to buck and can use their seat almost automatically to influence the horse against the idea. If caught unawares by a sudden buck, a good seat will keep the rider in the saddle and the problem is solved by riding strongly forwards into a slightly increased contact, making it clear to the horse that such behaviour is unacceptable. With this type of horse it is important to get and keep its attention, whether riding out or in the school, until its initial freshness has settled down. It is also worth looking at the diet and perhaps reducing the carbohydrate ration if the horse habitually has too much energy. Turning a stabled horse out for a while before riding will also help. If this is impossible, lungeing will work off excessive energy and is especially useful with young horses.

The horse that bucks to relieve pain or frustration is another matter. Badly fitting saddles, dirty girths and saddle pads that rub and chafe, or a physical problem which may cause the horse pain when ridden should all be ruled out. If none of these is the cause, then rider problems must be considered. The more people that ride a horse, the more opportunities the horse has to become confused and to try out evasions. Riding school horses, for example, have more opportunity than most to develop a repertoire of evasions to fool the inexperienced rider and bucking may be one of these. Once a horse has discovered how to buck and what the effects often are, it needs to be re-trained by an experienced rider who can both cope with the bucking and give the horse clear and correct aids, riding it forwards and showing it that bucking is not permitted and, in any case, will not have the desired effect.

You can usually sense if a horse is about to buck by the feeling of its back humping under you. Before that, it has to get its head down, which is not difficult if the horse is being ridden on a loose or uneven contact. Two aids to prevention, therefore, are to keep a steady contact and to keep your seat in the saddle. If you sense a buck coming on, ride the horse forwards, maintaining the contact. If you are too late and the buck happens anyway, sit up – you will have a better chance of staying on. Get the horse's head up and the moment you can, ride forwards, still keeping your seat firmly in the saddle. Keep riding and, if you are in the school, ride into a series of circles and changes of rein to get the horse concentrating on you and take its mind off bucking. In trot, be careful to sit up, in a correct position and avoid being pulled forwards if the horse tries to get its head down.

If you are not confident enough to cope, get some experienced help. This problem is not too difficult to solve, but it does need a capable rider.

Rearing: in hand

Cause

A horse that persistently rears in hand for no good reason, for example, when being brought in from the field, needs similar re-training to the horse that barges, since the problem is fundamentally one of disrespect. Maybe this horse has discovered that by rearing it can get away from a previous handler.

Solving the problem

A chifney bit will control the problem but re-training with the horse in a controller halter with a long leadrope is the best long-term solution. This is preferably done in a safe, controlled environment by a person experienced in lungeing and training young horses, who can react instantaneously to the horse's behaviour. The principle is that the horse should be kept moving since it needs to hesitate in order to rear. When it tries, a sharp tug on the halter will bring it back down, when it must instantly be led or driven forwards. The process must be continued until the horse goes forwards freely and confidently. Several sessions should be enough to resolve the problem.

Rearing: when ridden

Cause

This is really a variation of napping, that is, the horse has found a way to avoid going forwards and for the same variety of reasons.

Solving the problem

The solutions are also similar – remove the cause of any pain or discomfort, build up the horse's confidence if fear is the cause and acclimatise it to strange objects. When the rearing is due to disrespect, a return to the school to reinforce the horse's basic training to go forwards is needed.

To sit a rear, the rider should immediately give the rein and lean forwards to the side of the horse's neck. Inexperienced riders worry about the horse going over backwards but this is unlikely, unless the horse is encumbered by the rider virtually pulling it over. Leaning forwards puts your weight on the horse's front end which discourages it from going excessively high and shortens the time it stays up, while giving the rein ensures it can get its head back down. As the horse comes down, take back the contact and ride strongly forwards before it has time to consider a repeat performance.

None of the extreme methods suggested for

curing rearers are effective. Punishment with whip or spurs is equally useless since the horse is more likely to associate the punishment with whatever inclined it to rear in the first place, that is, it does not like the situation in which it finds itself. Correction must be firm, but it must be sympathetic and the horse must be able to understand what the rider is trying to communicate.

Pulling

Cause

The usual response to the pulling horse is to use a 'stronger' bit, so that if the horse becomes strong, the rider can hurt the horse more by pulling back. Let it be understood that no bit was ever designed to be used in such a way.

Horses do not pull against the rider unless the rider allows it. What happens first is that the rider may not have a secure and independent seat. This gives the horse the potential to get on the forehand and go faster, which it does when there is something exciting to tempt it, such as company or a nice open stretch of grass. The rider then begins to feel their lack of control and to worry about the speed, and so tries to slow the horse down by pulling back on the reins. Although its mouth is sensitive, to a horse with adrenaline pumping through its veins this is just a minor annoyance which it can easily deal with by tugging its head forwards to get it free again, or just lowering it and setting its jaw against the bit.

An ordinary snaffle does not have the potential to alter the horse's head carriage or get its attention long enough to stop it in such a situation, hence the move to a 'stronger' bit.

Solving the problem

The cure for the problem of pulling is schooling for the rider to improve first their seat and then their ability to apply effective aids. If a long-term battle has been waged, the horse must also be re-schooled patiently to remedy incorrect muscle development, typified by a large bulge along the underside of the neck.

There are, however, situations in which using a bit other than the ordinary snaffle is appropriate. In competitive situations, such as cross-country riding, or endurance, it may be necessary to have a way of getting the horse's attention when it is excited, or over enthusiastic. The choice of bit will depend upon exactly what the horse does (e.g., lean on the bit, snatch at the reins, etc.) and upon the shape and size of its mouth and the conformation of its head, neck and shoulders. The techniques employed to control the horse may vary slightly according to the bit choice (e.g., raising the hands with a gag), but they never depend upon pulling on the reins. In all cases, the rider's seat remains the main means of controlling the horse's movement, while the bit makes a momentary request from the rider's correctly carried hands. The request may need to be made repeatedly, but it must never be prolonged. Pulling steadily on a bit has only one result: it causes initial pain followed by deadening of the nerves. The horse's reaction is at first to pull back harder to get away from the pain and then to ignore the numbness.

Bolting

Cause

The natural response of a frightened horse is to run, but it does not usually run far. A horse which panics and bolts with its rider may not go more than a few strides before stopping, although if it thinks the cause of its fear is after it, for example, if a loosened brushing boot is 'snapping at its heels' or a lunge line is flapping behind it, it may continue to run until impending exhaustion brings it back to focus on the rider or handler.

Solving the problem

The worst danger when a horse bolts is that it may not even see obstacles in its way, such as fences or traffic and there is a serious risk of a nasty accident. It therefore becomes imperative to stop the horse as quickly as possible. If you are on its back, the only hope of stopping a committed bolter is to pull it round with one rein on a tight circle. Be aware that a slippery or uneven ground surface may cause the horse to stumble or fall when you do this and be prepared to leap off if necessary. Another possibility is to turn the horse into a thick hedge so that the bushes in its face bring it up short. The same does not apply to fences, which are insubstantial, or to solid walls, which would cause injury in the event of a crashing halt. Fortunately, bolting with this degree of risk rarely occurs and when it does, the solution is accident limitation, rather than schooling.

A lesser form of bolting, with the horse running away due to excitement or being startled and then refusing to stop because it is enjoying the gallop, is more common. Being run away with is not a pleasant experience and tends to linger in the memory. Of the four occasions on which I recall it happening to me, two were due to a steady training canter with another horse turning into a race between them, with neither taking any notice of their riders. On both occasions I was trying out a horse, previously unknown to me, having been invited to ride in endurance races abroad. Neither horse was adequately schooled and both were in ordinary snaffle bits. Both were on high-energy diets and neither had been given sufficient work to merit the quantity of feed. I stopped the first by turning it in a tight circle into soft sand in the desert and the second by doing the same into a ploughed field.

The moral of these experiences is that well-schooled, obedient horses with an appropriate regime of work and feed do not behave in this way, first, because they have learned to trust and listen to their rider and, second, because they do not have the added excuse of limited freedom and excessive energy.

Mounting problems

Cause

The most usual problem encountered when mounting is that of the horse moving off before you are in the saddle. Anything more violent, such as the horse rearing, going down on its knees or dropping its back from under you, is most likely related to existing pain, or a past painful experience. This could be anything from a saddle that pinches to a severely damaged back and the

If you are on your own, putting the horse in a corner will make mounting easier.

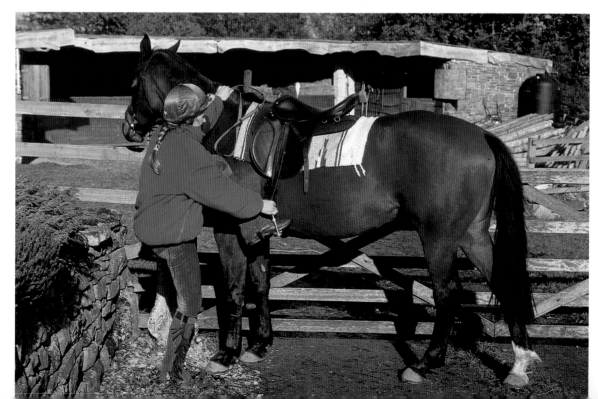

Once up, Becky insists that Tammy stands, before she moves off.

cause must be diagnosed and resolved before the horse is ridden further.

Solving the problem

Patience is needed to cope with the horse that moves off. First be sure that the rider is not asking the horse to move by inadvertently jabbing a toe into its ribs or causing other discomfort. Ideally use a mounting block. Begin simply by asking the horse to stand quietly at the mounting block without trying to mount. This is best done after lungeing, for example, when the horse is not too fresh and impatient. Lead it away and back and repeat the process until it gets the idea. All this work can be done alone, but a helper to discourage the horse from moving by standing in front of it and, perhaps, raising a hand in front of its face, may be useful.

Next progress to asking the horse to stand while you climb on to the mounting block. Stroke the horse and praise it for standing still, then lead it away again. Repeat until the lesson is established.

Finally, ask the horse to stand while you mount from the block. Stay quiet and allow the horse's head some freedom. Picking up the reins to a short length just encourages it to move off. Mount carefully, making sure to keep your toe down and to swing your other leg quietly clear of the horse's back. Sit still, stroke and praise the horse, then pick up your reins and ask the horse to step forwards. If it moves off before you are fully mounted, bring it quietly back to the mounting block and ask it to stand. Dismount and repeat the exercise.

An alternative method, which is probably less effective long term, but gives you enough opportunity to mount then immediately move off, is to face the horse into the corner of a paddock or arena, so there is an obstacle to prevent it from moving. However, horses are adept at turning quickly on a sixpence and will do so before you can settle yourself fully in the saddle.

Resistance to the bit

Cause

This can have many causes and occur in varying degrees. First, dental problems must be ruled out. Next, consider the size and thickness of the bit in relation to the conformation of the horse's mouth. A small mouth is uncomfortable with too thick a bit. A low palate reacts with pain to the nutcracker action of a single-jointed bit. Too thin a bit may cut into thicker fleshy bars and lips.

Next, look at the horse's head carriage, conformation of head and neck and way of going and consider how that changes with the rider on board.

Solving the problem

Choose an appropriate bit for the circumstances. A rubber snaffle is very useful for rehabilitating a badly or roughly trained horse's mouth. The softer, synthetic bits, such as the 'happy mouth' range are also useful and give more variety in terms of thickness and shape of mouthpiece. A horse that goes above the bit, in a hollow outline, often with a ewe neck and heavy muscle development on the underside, should respond well to a pelham used with two reins. This would be inappropriate, however, for the horse that puts its head down, tucks in its chin and leans on the bit. In this case, a bit with rollers, which discourages leaning and encourages salivation, is useful.

If not pain induced, resistance is usually rider induced and the appropriate choice of bit, coupled with correct, balanced riding, will make re-training easier.

Getting the tongue over the bit is a common problem, especially with young horses, which play with the bit a good deal in the early stages of ridden work. Sometimes, it occurs because the handler has fitted the bit slightly too low in an attempt to minimise pressure on the tender corners of the young horse's mouth. In other cases, a change of bit, for example, to a straight-bar, mullen-mouth, or slightly ported bit will resolve the problem. Even switching from a single-jointed to a French link snaffle may be sufficient. The remedy consists, first, of minimising the horse's ability to get its tongue over the bit and, second, of breaking the habit of trying to do it. As a temporary measure, therefore, a flash or drop noseband, which helps keep the mouth closed, will help. The remedy is reinforced by careful schooling, encouraging the horse to concentrate on work and to reach for and accept the bit rather than trying to evade or get rid of it.

Personality problems

Cause

Sometimes, a horse's habitual behaviour changes for no apparent reason. The calm, equable horse takes to bucking or charging off. The horse that is normally pleasant to deal with becomes a tyrant in the stable. A forward-going mare starts napping or becomes dull and wooden to ride. Why do these things happen?

Solving the problem

In the case of the mare, the oestrus cycle is often to blame and the mare in season becomes distracted and irritable, or just disinterested in work. In particularly difficult cases hormone treatment can help.

The calm horse that suddenly becomes playful or unmanageable is likely suffering from a surfeit of spring grass. Many owners are happy to see new grass but forget that the extra nourishment it provides means that the concentrate ration can be reduced.

Finally, the horse that becomes bad tempered for no apparent reason will have a reason, although it might take you a while to discover it. A relatively common cause is dislike of the horse stabled next door and behaviour changes may occur when a horse is moved from adjoining a liked companion to a stranger, particularly, for example, if the new next-door neighbour is dominant when the horses are turned out in the field, or of a different sex. We have three adjoining boxes which have only half height partitions separating them. Most of our horses are quite happy to be next door to other members of the family, but one mare, whose separate stable had to be temporarily vacated, reacted badly to this 'open plan' living and resorted to biting and other displays of aggression, whenever a human entered the stable. As soon as the neighbouring horse was turned out her normal, friendly temperament reappeared.

Conclusion

Whenever you have a specific problem with a horse, the solution should follow the same pattern. First, analyse the cause and treat or resolve any physical problems or pain. Second, if the cause is not physical, analyse the reasons for it and resolve them. Third, patiently show the horse that the reasons for the problematic behaviour no longer exist and win back its confidence in you and in its own ability to do as you ask. Finally, reinforce the re-training and correct response with repetition, praise and reward.

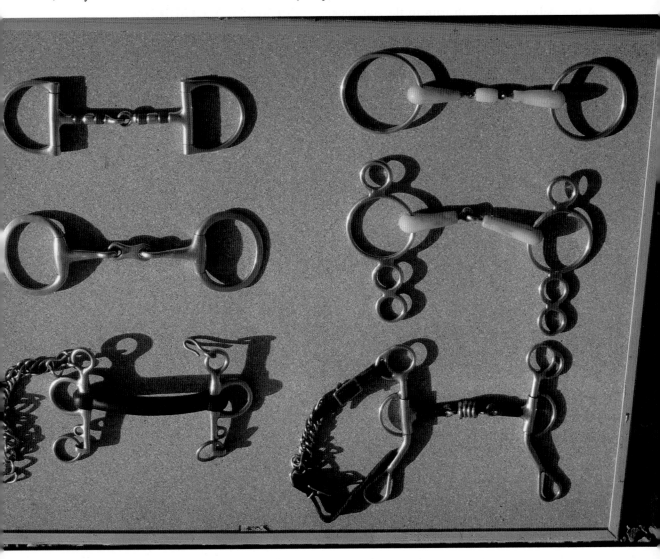

Some bits in regular use on our yard:

(Left from top) Snaffle with copper rollers; French link Snaffle; Mullen mouth pelham;

(Right from top) 'Peanut' Happy Mouth Snaffle; Happy Mouth Dutch gag; Western reining bit (used in endurance competitions).

Chapter 13

Gadgets

Although there are usually four or five horses being worked in our yard at any one time, our tack room is remarkable for its minimalist flavour. It contains the following working gear:

- **Three saddles**
- **Five bridles with cavesson nosebands**
- **Two hunting breastplates**
- **Ten bits including a hackamore**
- **One flash noseband**
- **One grakle noseband**
- **One standing martingale**
- **One running martingale**
- **One lungeing cavesson**
- **One pair of side reins**
- **One chambon**
- **Two lunge lines**
- **One Newmarket coupling**
- **One breaking roller with breastplate**
- **One 'natural horsemanship' halter**
- **One 'be nice' halter**
- **Four headcollars**
- **Three sets of brushing boots**
- **Three sets of over-reach boots**
- **Saddle pads and blankets**

For schooling and training at home our competition horses wear their own saddle with a breastplate, as we spend a lot of time in the mountains, plus a snaffle bridle. Brushing boots are used for schooling and for riding out on young horses before their muscles have strengthened. For endurance competitions, we may change the bit to counteract any tendency to over enthusiasm, selecting a bit that suits the horse and in which it goes well. Our third saddle is used for breaking and basic schooling of youngsters.

In many tackrooms you will find a martingale with every bridle, as a matter of course. We believe, however, that all extra aids should only be used when required, for specific purposes.

For example, a running martingale is useful for safety when jumping or riding cross-country to prevent a horse from evading the rider's rein aids by getting above the bit and perhaps crashing into a fence. It has no place in schooling. A standing martingale is handy for a nervous horse that has been frightened and is being re-trained. Like the running martingale, it prevents the horse from getting above the bit and thus helps keep its attention on the rider, whilst discouraging any tendency to run, but also has the advantage of not interfering with the action of the bit.

A flash noseband can be useful for a young horse that opens its mouth or tries to grab hold of the bit and chew it, instead of mouthing it softly. The presence of wolf teeth should be ruled out, however, before you resort to its use. It also helps a little in encouraging the horse to lower its head in response to the rein aids and begin to develop a steady head carriage. The grakle is useful for a horse that gets strong and sets its jaw across country. For regular riding on a trained horse, a cavesson noseband (or none at all) should suffice.

There are various books available on the use of other specific training aids (see Further Reading), but basically the purpose of any training aid is to encourage the horse to use its body in a way that will help it develop correctly with the aim of carrying a rider. Incorrect and inhumane uses include any attempts to force the horse into assuming an outline it is not ready to adopt, or any means of tying the head into a specific position. All training aids should be used with circumspection and due attention to the level of training the horse has reached, its conformation and potential for achieving the desired work and as a means of encouragement and guidance, not of resistance and force. Unfortunately, even in well meaning hands, the use of training aids often falls well below this objective. If you want to pursue your horse training

ambitions to this level, you need to train your own eyes to be observant and to understand the physiology of the horse and the dynamics of movement, as well as the theory of the use of the equipment involved.

The twitch as a method of restraint

The twitch is a device commonly used to subdue a horse that becomes fractious when being treated in some way, whether for veterinary treatment, farriery or other management practices.

The home-made version consists simply of a loop of string, threaded through some sort of handle, usually a stout stick about 45 cm (18 in) long. The loop is placed over the sensitive end of the nose and the stick twisted to tighten the string. A manufactured 'humane twitch', which resembles a large pair of metal nutcrackers, can also be purchased. The latter works in the same way, but is designed to prevent over-tightening and cutting off the circulation.

The standing martingale, adjusted so that it only comes into play when the horse goes above the bit.

The chambon is one of many available schooling aids. It comes into play when the horse raises its head, so is useful for encouraging it to stretch forward and down.

It was originally thought that the pain of the twitch caused the horse to stand still. However, it is now known that the application of the twitch causes the release of endorphins, so the twitch can justifiably be used as a humane means of restraint, although its application is still unpleasant for the horse. Unfortunately, the twitch is often used as a shortcut to coping with a problem, instead of the handler spending the time and having the patience to desensitise the horse to whatever is required so that it accepts it with equanimity. Examples might be clipping, or pulling the mane. Stable managers also often resort to the twitch in a last attempt to carry out a procedure, before going to the expense of calling in the vet to sedate the horse.

As a veterinary surgeon, Tony rarely uses the twitch, preferring to treat the horse without restraint if possible. His most likely application is when a horse that resents injections requires a repeated course over an extended period. Since sedation requires an injection anyway, the twitch is the easiest and least unpleasant recourse. Some vets may twitch a horse to give routine vaccinations if the horse is considered to be difficult, but Tony would do this only in extreme circumstances. His approach is to win the horse's confidence and he is invariably able to give the injection without trauma for either the horse or the owner.

Another application of the twitch might be when dressings on a painful wound have to be changed on a daily basis and repeated sedation would be both detrimental to the horse and expensive.

In summary, the twitch is a useful tool for specific difficult circumstances, but it should not be used routinely as an alternative to patient habituation and desensitisation of the horse to routine, non-invasive management procedures.

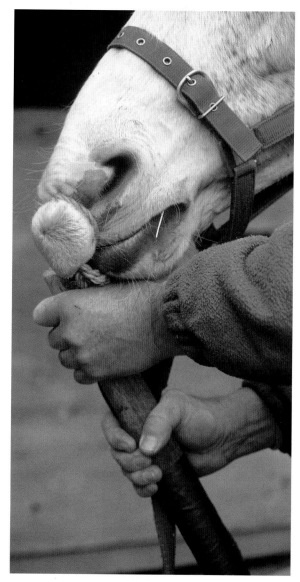

A twitch.

Chapter 14

Re-educating the Mistreated Horse

Some horses are ill treated through deliberate acts of malice. Others suffer abuse through ignorance or thoughtlessness, while many more are confused and behave inappropriately due to their handlers' lack of understanding and inability to communicate in a way the horse can understand, even though they may mean well and want to do their best for the horse.

Whatever the cause of the trouble, the route back to acceptable 'good' behaviour and the horse being able to lead a useful, productive life is invariably the same. The degree to which you can hope for success in retraining and rehabilitating an abused horse depends not only upon the skill and dedication of the trainer, but also on how severely the horse was traumatised in the first place. Remember that horses have long memories and can become habituated as easily to 'bad' as to 'good' behaviour. Even when re-trained, such a horse might revert to its old, unacceptable reactions if startled, upset, or inconsiderately handled in the future.

A trainer we knew regularly took on horses that had defeated other people's efforts. One was an Arabian gelding that became invaluable as a school horse for students. 'If you do not ride him properly, he simply goes on strike,' the trainer explained. This horse could perform advanced dressage movements but, if ridden with the slightest lack of sympathy, it balked and refused to go forwards. If

Abuse takes many forms. Starvation is just one of them.

pressed, it would drop a shoulder and deposit the rider in the arena. Many people would consider a horse like this to be badly behaved, but the trainer realised that the horse was both intelligent and very sensitive and, having learnt its evasions with previous owners, would no longer tolerate the discomfort of poor riding. The horse led a happy and useful life for years as a schoolmaster, before being retired with one of its student riders.

Another horse owned by the same trainer had been broken roughly with a wire bit and then passed through the hands of several people who had tried and failed to school it. Our trainer re-schooled it from the beginning using classical methods and the horse learned to accept the bit and work well, provided it was ridden with very soft hands. Any inadvertent pressure on its mouth, however, would send it into a violent bucking fit until the rider was off. This story shows that a horse's past experiences can never be ignored and that it is essential to find out as much as possible about its history before you attempt to resolve a problem. Some horses, such as this one, will always need a high standard of riding technique and, in the wrong hands, can be dangerous.

Removing the cause

The first step in rehabilitating any badly treated horse is to find out what stimulus causes the undesirable behaviour and remove it. This may be as drastic as rescuing the horse from mistreatment or abuse and transferring it to a new, happier environment. It may be as simple as changing its stable to one with a different view, or changing its next-door neighbour. In some cases, actual physical pain may be to blame. Something as simple as a wolf tooth, or a badly fitted saddle, may cause pain when the horse is ridden and, naturally, the horse reacts by trying to get rid of what it perceives as the cause of its pain, in this case the rider.

Pain may be more insidious, due to an injury that has gone unnoticed, with subtle symptoms that may need veterinary diagnosis. Therefore, just because you cannot see an obvious cause for bad behaviour, do not assume there is none. A horse does not have to be hopping with lameness to be in pain.

Mental anguish is another form of pain and one that may have many causes, from straightforward fear of a rough handler to less obvious stress due to being over-faced, or competed excessively, or the confusion of conflicting signals from an inexperienced rider.

How severely a horse responds to inappropriate handling depends upon the nature and sensitivity of the individual horse. For example, a pony with a painful mouth or back might try to run away from the pain and become dubbed a 'puller' as the rider resorts to ever harder hands in an attempt to apply brakes. A sensitive young Thoroughbred or Anglo-Arab might take to bucking in response to confusing requests from over enthusiastic legs combined with heavy hands. A horse that is frustrated by a handler who is too rough in grooming or girthing up might bite or kick. A nervous horse that has been frightened or misused by a rider with a whip might throw its head up and try to bolt. The list of possibilities is endless and the trainer's skill lies in regaining the horse's trust, understanding what caused the problem, then showing it progressively that there is nothing to fear or react against.

Rest and rehabilitation

Once the cause of a problem has been removed, the horse must be allowed time to relax and settle before re-training commences. Often, horses with problems are passed from one person to another in the hope of finding a solution, with each handler trying something different in a new and different environment. The horse may be very stressed by this succession of changes so that it is no longer certain where home is and does not have a reliable partnership with any one person. To say the least, it is confused, probably weary and also possibly nervous and afraid of what might happen next. If physical pain was the cause of the difficulty, it is almost certainly also stiff and sore, its muscles tight and contracted from incorrect use or in compensation for a particular injury or ailment.

It is therefore very important to allow sufficient time for recuperation before attempting a re-training programme. If possible, the horse should be turned out to grass day and night, with companions nearby, if not in the same pasture. It should be allowed to rest and relax, so that the tensions can ease out of the muscles and damaged tissue has time to repair. If extra food is needed, it should be of good nutritional quality and designed to put on condition without producing excessive energy. Horses that have been mistreated or over-stressed often lack good health and condition. The musculature may be sunken rather than rounded and the coat dull or staring. Any routine veterinary or farriery needs should be attended to during this recuperation period.

The handler who is going to re-train the horse should visit it in the field, ideally two or three times a day, to bring food and also to observe the horse's behaviour, begin to get acquainted with it and encourage its trust.

The length of time needed for this period of physical and mental recuperation depends upon what happened to the horse, how severely traumatised it is, whether it needs to recover from an actual injury, its temperament and what basic condition it is in on arrival. The appropriate period might be anything from a few days to weeks or even months. In most cases, where the situation is not determined by physical condition, the horse's attitude will show when it is ready to begin work. An anxious horse will often stand by the gate, or move restlessly around the field rather than graze steadily and quietly. We once had one that spent three days walking the perimeter of its field before it finally discovered the joys of grass. Apparently this horse had spent most of its ten years in a livery yard without ever being turned out to graze. A horse should be relaxed when out at grass, alternately grazing, dozing, wandering around or lying down. When the horse begins to recognise the handler's approach and looks forward to their visits, coming up to the gate with its ears pricked, that is an encouraging sign. If it is happy to stand while hands are run over its body, then shows a tendency to follow when the handler walks away, the horse is paying attention and ready to listen.

The re-training programme

A young horse, being schooled for the first time, will try out various evasions that can be nipped in the bud if handled correctly. An older horse, with a history of mistreatment, may have learned a variety of responses to various stimuli, which result in it evading the handler's control. Even with a full history available, it is difficult to anticipate exactly when and how these incidents are likely to happen. Often, the horse's past history and the roots of a behavioural problem are unknown. It is therefore extremely important that re-training is broken down into small, logical steps and is very thorough.

The first essential is to build up the horse's developing, but still wary, trust in the handler. This is best done by steady, systematic exposure of the horse to the handler's presence. For the first few days of working with an anxious or nervous horse, desensitisation of the horse to the handler's presence in the stable and their movements around the horse's body are all that should be attempted. A few days of gentle grooming, fingertip massage and getting the horse accustomed to your way of moving around it, your smell and your voice can work wonders.

Progress from this point depends upon the nature of the problem, but time spent in going through the basics is never wasted. Everything should be done calmly, naturally, and considerately and the horse's reactions observed. From grooming, progress is made to tacking up, to leading out in hand, to lungeing or long reining and, eventually, to riding.

Consideration must be given to the choice of equipment and the horse's reaction to it. Ensure that the saddle fits comfortably and choose a milder bit in preference to a stronger one. Whenever the horse is reluctant or refuses to accept any part of basic training, the reaction must be observed, the reason worked out and time spent on correcting that issue. Neglecting to do so in order to tackle a more advanced ridden problem just leaves a gap in the horse's education that will always be there. It is often found that when the basics are correctly re-established, the more difficult ridden problem miraculously disappears – the horse no longer needs to evade, because finally it has learned to carry a rider without discomfort. Unless the horse receives a reminder, in some way, of the pain, frustration or confusion it previously endured, there is no need for it to repeat previous 'bad' behaviour.

Conclusion

Many people assume that curing a horse of bad behaviour involves waiting for the behaviour to occur and then punishing the horse for it, usually with the whip, possibly with spurs and probably with a lot of shouting. In fact, such treatment is not only ineffectual, but also very likely to make the situation much worse. Horses never learn anything from negative training. By the time you try to tell them 'That is bad – do not do it!' you are already too late. Also, the more often a horse succeeds in making the wrong move, the more that move is reinforced and the more often it will repeat it in future.

It is not surprising that the same theory applies to human learning. When we remind ourselves over and over again of how we failed at something, we increase our chances of failing again next time. Unfortunately for us, we are far more likely to dwell on what we did wrong, for example, in a dressage test or on the cross-country course, than what we did right. If, however, we concentrated our thoughts on how we did something well, we would increase our chances of getting it right again.

The only way to train, or re-train a horse is through positive learning and reinforcement. For example, the key to curing a horse's tendency to buck, once any valid reason for the behaviour such as a pinching saddle has been removed, is to ride it in such a way that its inclination to buck is anticipated and prevented before the buck actually occurs. The horse discovers, first, that the rider's secure seat discourages the habit by making it more difficult for the horse to position itself for a buck and, second, that it has no real reason to buck because it is no longer experiencing any discomfort. Through the repetition of the positive experience of being ridden well and in comfort, the horse progressively realises that the stimulus that caused it to buck has disappeared and it is, in fact, easier and more pleasant

not to buck. In a relatively short time, positive good riding can overcome the habit of bucking.

On the other hand, if the rider fails to ride with a secure, balanced seat but perches nervously forwards, the horse will find it very easy to get its head down and continue the habit of bucking. Assuming the rider manages not to fall off, if they then punish the horse with the whip, the horse will continue to associate being ridden with discomfort, and so react with a buck, or resort to some other evasion, such as napping, whenever it is unhappy.

Another piece of advice sometimes given to less experienced riders is to 'tire the horse out' to cure over-excitable or unmanageable behaviour. We recently heard of someone who did this on a very hot day and galloped the horse to the point where it collapsed with exhaustion. Only expert, prompt veterinary attention saved the horse's life. Horses that behave like this usually need less high-energy food and more exercise at home, coupled with a more gradual introduction to increasingly exciting show or event environments. Galloping, or forcing such a horse to work beyond the level to which it is trained just to get rid of natural exuberance does not effect a permanent cure and is very likely to do irreparable damage to the legs.

This story serves to reinforce the fact that there are no shortcuts in horse training. If you truly love horses, you should never need to look for any, since the fascination of achieving successful progress, with each small step along the way, is more than enough reward in itself.

Further Reading

Useful Addresses

Getting in Touch with Horses,
Linda Tellington-Jones, Kenilworth Press Ltd,
1995

Natural Horse-man-ship,
Pat Parelli, Western Horseman Inc,
1993

Centred Riding,
Sally Swift, Trafalgar Square Farm,
1985

BodySense,
Sally A. Tottle, The Kenilworth Press Ltd,
1998

Imprint Training of the Newborn Foal,
Robert M. Miller DVM, Western Horseman Inc,
1991

The Nature of Horses,
Stephen Budiansky, Weidenfeld & Nicolson,
1997

The Horse's Mind,
Lucy Rees, Stanley Paul & Co. Ltd,
1984

Saddlery,
Elwyn Hartley Edwards, J. A. Allen & Company,
1963

Training Aids in Theory and Practice,
Elwyn Hartley Edwards, J. A. Allen & Company,
1990

Lungeing and Long-Reining,
Jennie Loriston-Clarke, The Kenilworth Press Ltd,
1993

Farriers Registration Council,
PO Box 49, East of England Showground,
Peterborough, Cambridgeshire, PE2 6GU.
Tel: 01733 371171

**International League for the
Protection of Horses,**
Anne Colvin House, Hall Farm, Snetterton,
Norwich, Norfolk, NR16 2LR.
Tel: 01953 498682

National Foaling Bank,
Meretown Stud, Newport, Shropshire, TF10 8BX.
Tel: 01952 811234

Royal College of Veterinary Surgeons,
Belgravia House, 62–64 Horseferry Road,
London, SW1P 2AF.
Tel: 0171 222 2001

Index